PREACH
AND HEAL

A Biblical Model for Missions

CHARLES FIELDING, M.D.

PREACH
AND HEAL

A Biblical Model for Missions

ISBN-13: 978-0-9767645-6-4

Published by the International Mission Board, Richmond, Virginia

Dewey Decimal Classification: 266

Subject Heading: FOREIGN MISSIONS
Unless otherwise noted, all Scripture quotations are taken from the Holman Christian Standard Bible® Copyright © 1999, 2000, 2002, 2003 by Holman Bible Publishers. Used by permission. Holman Christian Standard Bible®, Holman CSB®, and HCSB® are federally registered trademarks of Holman Bible Publishers.
Cover and interior design: Susan Browne Design, Nashville, TN
Editor: Kim P. Davis, Richmond, VA

12 RRD 9 8 7 6

For M and every apostolic worker
who has dedicated her or his life
to the advancement of God's kingdom.

CONTENTS

ACKNOWLEDGMENTS

Over the years, I have been taught a thousand lessons by dozens of teachers. For the sake of security, it is best that I not mention names or even tell where I learned these lessons. But I must thank the many people, from many countries and from varied backgrounds, who have enabled me to pass on their knowledge in this book.

I would also like to thank my wife, M, and my children, C and MG. We are a family team for Jesus, and they empower me through their prayers and encouragement.

Mostly, I am indebted to my Savior. His blood has purchased my passage into His kingdom and through His peace and partnership in His power, our family has found our obligation to the nations to be a blessing rather than a burden.

Charles Fielding, M.D.

FOREWORD

Mission history has been replete with an unfortunate tension between evangelism and social ministry. Obviously there have been those who have sought to proclaim the life-transforming message of the Gospel while ignoring the suffering and physical needs of their listeners. Likewise, there have been those who confined their witness to the good works they might do while never offering the recipients spiritual hope.

Our Lord makes it clear that neglecting either one is not an option for the faithful and obedient disciple. Wherever Jesus went, He responded to human needs. He gave sight to the blind, cleansed the leper, healed the lame, and raised the dead, though the primary purpose of His coming was to provide deliverance and salvation for those in sin.

Jesus not only modeled love and compassion toward the less fortunate, He commanded us to love our neighbors and help those in need. He also demanded repentance from sin as essential to entering the kingdom of God, and we should not seek to improve the quality of life of those upon earth without also providing them hope of life after death.

Preach and Heal is a testimony and practical manual that eliminates any pretext of a dichotomy between evangelism and compassionate ministries. The author is a doctor who is passionate about people coming to faith in Jesus Christ. He has served in the remotest locations of countries restricted to a Christian witness, yet with integrity and boldness, he has shared his faith while skillfully meeting human needs. His years of experience are reflected in his diversity of approaches to minister and find acceptance in the most hostile environment. His book will give a new vision for touching a lost world with the love of Jesus Christ.

The needs are evident, both spiritual and physical, but it is not merely the need that leads one to give of himself. It is for the glory of God that one dares to walk in obedience, compelled by His love to preach and heal.

Jerry Rankin, *president*
International Mission Board, SBC

INTRODUCTION

At a conference for medical missionaries, I hit it off with a new worker serving in South Asia. We laughed over stories of our adventures in ministry. We were surrounded by dedicated health workers who had come to this conference to learn how to be the best possible doctors and dentists for Jesus Christ. At the first break, I found out just why he and I were hitting it off so well.

When we had gotten away from the crowd, he whispered, "I don't know how to say this, but I have a problem. I don't really feel like a doctor. I really feel like a church planter trapped inside the body of a doctor." I looked around to make sure no one was listening and whispered, "Yeah, me too."

My new friend's statement was politically incorrect. We are doctors, and doctors are meant to do doctoring stuff. Church planting is preacher's work and should be done by preachers. Can you imagine what would happen if we started mixing all of this up? Your gynecologist might read to you from the book of Lamentations, or your pastor, while shaking your hand, might check you for skin cancer. Nevertheless, that is what this book is about. My goal is to make church planters out of doctors and health practitioners out of preachers. Jesus practiced, taught, and commanded both. Church planting without care for the needy and healthcare without church planting are both forms of malpractice.

Health strategies *are not* dependent upon buildings, fancy equipment, or even doctors and nurses. Health strategies *are* for every disciple regardless of background. By ministering with loving hands to individuals and imparting the Gospel, the potential to transform entire communities ensues. This transformation can be the starting point for an indigenous movement of disciples and churches across entire regions.

By the end of the book, you should be able to design your own health strategy. Strategic thinking requires the ability to think outside of the traditional box. For this reason, I will be using some nontraditional terminology.

One term that I will not use often is "missionary." It isn't that this is a bad word, but the unevangelized people groups of the world are mostly located in countries that do not welcome missionaries. In their minds, a missionary is one who has judged their culture as inferior and wants to change every nation to be more like America and Western Europe. "Missionary" is the Latin translation of the biblical word "apostle." Therefore, when referring to one whom the Lord has sent to make disciples in an unevangelized region, I will use a term such as "apostolic worker" or "apostolic minister."

Another label that I use is "disciple" instead of "Christian." I live in the Middle East where the term "Christian" is related to Western politics. A Christian is seen as one who comes to destroy. A disciple is seen as an apolitical servant, which describes us more accurately.

Well, I think those are the two most noticeable peculiarities in the book, so I hope we now have an understanding. I feel sorry for the people that don't read the introduction.

PART ONE

Lectionary Homiletics
or Aesculapian Arts

(Preach or Heal)

CHAPTER 1

TWO CAMPS

Apostolic workers, otherwise known as "missionaries," can be divided into one of two camps: *preachers* or *healers*. It's easy to differentiate between them. Just ask what they are reading, what projects they are working on, and what their hopes are for the future. Within minutes you will know to which camp one belongs. If you don't get the information you desire, offer to pick up the check and you should get an earful.

Preachers love to preach, and they read books about preaching and teaching. They have insights into the workings of God and man and are particularly skilled at sharing those insights with others. Preachers put in long hours in their study followed by many hours with the nationals they are training. At the same time, they always are finding opportunities to teach, whether in a taxi or on an airplane.

Their focus seems to be on the whole community or city, and they dream up projects to teach nationals to evangelize others. They have slogans like "Winning our city for Christ," and they will talk to any audience about this subject. This is what they go to bed and wake up thinking about, what distracts them from their family time, and what they talk about when they get together. It is largely who they are. Their hope is to transform the community through the power of the Holy Spirit, starting with those they teach.

Healers love to heal, and they read books to hone their skills at healing. Because the communities that they serve have a variety of ills, healers have a variety of foci. They may be healing a poor educational system by teaching; healing an ailing economy by providing economic development; or healing physical, social, or emotional pains. They put in long hours with people, whether in a medical clinic, digging wells, teaching English, or teaching business practices. The nationals of the country use words like "compassionate" and "caring" to describe them, and these healers are not afraid to roll up their sleeves and get their hands dirty.

Their focus is on the individuals they see in their classrooms and clinics, and they have difficulty walking away from any person with a problem. They care deeply for those who are hurting or marginalized by society, and they dream up projects that help these needy people. This is what they think about, what distracts them from their family time, and what they talk about when they get together. It is largely who they are. Their hope is to transform the community through the power of the Holy Spirit, starting with the patients or students they have impacted through their services.

Both camps are passionate about their work, and, don't get me wrong, they do get along. In fact, generally neither preachers nor healers really are content with this dichotomy. But they don't know what to do about it. Preachers call healers when they need to fix something or their children are sick. Healers call preachers if they have questions about theology. They even understand a bit about the other. Yet deep down, they have a great love for their own area of expertise and wish the other could see how *their* ministry clearly makes a difference.

Personally, I am a medical doctor and have the capacity to put on a white coat and sit with those in the healer camp. However, I am also a church planter. I can easily take off the white coat, carry a Bible, and slip unnoticed into the preacher camp. Here are some notes that I have surreptitiously recorded while spying on each camp:

FROM THE HEALERS

Health and caring ministries are not optional for disciples of Jesus
Christ. As disciples, we are a reflection of Jesus. Christ within us, as
it says in Colossians 1:27, is the hope of glory for the nations. As we
demonstrate our love for others, people will see Jesus within us and
will turn to Him.

Jesus demonstrated His compassionate nature by feeding the
hungry; by healing the lame, the blind, the leper, the one suffering
from hemorrhage and seizures; by casting out demons; and by raising those who were paralyzed or even those who were dead. How
can we claim to be representatives of Jesus if we do not do the same
things that He did? When you think of Jesus, you must think of acts
of healing, love, and compassion. If we are to be a reflection of His
glory, then these same attributes must be seen by the nations in us,
or how can Christ be seen in us at all?

> In the same way, think about the great commandment.
> When asked: "'Teacher, which commandment in the law
> is the greatest?' He said to him, 'Love the Lord your God
> with all your heart, with all your soul, and with all your
> mind. This is the greatest and most important command-
> ment. The second is like it: Love your neighbor as your-
> self. All the Law and the Prophets depend on these two
> commandments'" (Matthew 22:36-40).

At another time, while explaining what it means to love one's
neighbor, Jesus told the story of the Good Samaritan, in which a man
cared for an injured stranger, even to the point of putting him up in a
hotel room and changing his bandages (Luke 10:29-37).

In the Great Commission, Jesus further commanded the disciples to "go, therefore, and make disciples of all nations… *teaching*
them to observe everything I have commanded you" (Matthew
28:19-20; italics mine). Even in these parting words, Jesus reminds
His disciples to remember His teachings and commands. As they
and we multiply, we must teach all disciples to obey the command to
care for the needy.

FROM THE PREACHERS

You must remember the basics. Jesus taught that "you always have the poor with you" (Mark 14:7a). All of the social services in the world will never be able to stem the tide of suffering on this earth. Every life that is saved through these expensive services will still end up dying and, without the Gospel, will enter into hell. Your intention to help a hurting world is admirable, but Robert Coleman said, "One cannot transform a world except as individuals in the world are transformed, and individuals cannot be changed except as they are molded in the hands of the Master."[1]

It sounds mean, but do you get the point? It is good that you care about individuals, but people are transformed in the "hands of the Master," not in your healing hands.

Furthermore, the very return of Christ is contingent upon preaching. "This good news of the kingdom will be proclaimed in all the world as a testimony to all nations. And then the end will come" (Matthew 24:14). These nations cannot know and cannot turn to God unless they hear the message of salvation. Remember what it says in Romans 10:14: "But how can they call on Him in whom they have not believed? And how can they believe without hearing about Him? And how can they hear without a preacher?"

It is impossible, and not biblical, to try to alleviate every physical and social ill of society. The only hope for the communities to which we are ministering is in the power of the Gospel "because it is God's power for salvation to everyone who believes" (Romans 1:16b). The power of social services is negligible compared to this.

THE HEALERS AGAIN

How can we, with the resources to help the needy, just pass by the masses that are dying? As James 2:15-16 says: "If a brother or sister is without clothes and lacks daily food, and one of you says to them, 'Go in peace, keep warm, and eat well,' but you don't give them what the body needs, what good is it?" The world is full of hurting people and they need us. Healing ministries have been helping people from the beginning days of Christianity, and God has demonstrated His support for us by enabling us to do much for the poor and needy.

The very basic teachings of Jesus are that those who have been blessed with goods must share with those who are in need. As Luke 12:48 says: "Much will be required of everyone who has been given much. And even more will be expected of the one who has been entrusted with more."

NOW THE PREACHERS AGAIN

Saint Paul's method was to enter into a town, go to the synagogue, and preach the Gospel. Can't those healers read the Bible? Just think of the verses that uphold the value of preaching:

> So faith comes from what is heard, and what is heard comes through the message about Christ (Romans 10:17).

> For if I preach the gospel, I have no reason to boast, because an obligation is placed on me. And woe to me if I do not preach the gospel! (1 Corinthians 9:16)

> Until I come, give your attention to public reading, exhortation, and teaching (1 Timothy 4:13).

Paul's bottom line to Timothy was "proclaim the message; persist in it whether convenient or not; rebuke, correct, and encourage with great patience and teaching" (2 Timothy 4:2). Preaching the Word must be our focus and what we model to the nationals so that it will become a part of the culture of the indigenous church.

THE HEALERS, COMING BACK AT THEM

Okay, I heard that. Yes, we do know our Bible, perhaps a bit better than you think. You preachers put so much emphasis on what you can see in this material world. You preach about spiritual truth, but you are obsessed with counting the things that you can touch with your hands. You count preaching points and baptisms and conversions. Are you so sure that that is the proper measure of success for a man or for the church?

If you want to look at Scripture, then look at the last sermon given by Jesus in the book of Matthew. It explains simply what is important to Jesus and how He will judge the success of a man's life.

When the Son of Man comes in His glory, and all the angels with Him, then He will sit on the throne of His glory. All the nations will be gathered before Him, and He will separate them one from another, just as a shepherd separates the sheep from the goats. He will put the sheep on His right, and the goats on the left. Then the King will say to those on His right, "Come, you who are blessed by My Father, inherit the kingdom prepared for you from the foundation of the world.

"For I was hungry and you gave Me something to eat; I was thirsty and you gave Me something to drink; I was a stranger and you took Me in;

"I was naked and you clothed Me; I was sick and you took care of Me; I was in prison and you visited Me."

Then the righteous will answer Him, "Lord, when did we see You hungry and feed You, or thirsty and give You something to drink? When did we see You a stranger and take You in, or without clothes and clothe You? When did we see You sick, or in prison, and visit You?"

And the King will answer them, "I assure you: Whatever you did for one of the least of these brothers of Mine, you did for Me." Then He will also say to those on the left, "Depart from Me, you who are cursed, into the eternal fire prepared for the Devil and his angels!

"For I was hungry and you gave Me nothing to eat; I was thirsty and you gave Me nothing to drink; I was a stranger and you didn't take Me in; I was naked and you didn't clothe Me, sick and in prison and you didn't take care of Me."

Then they too will answer, "Lord, when did we see You hungry, or thirsty, or a stranger, or without clothes, or sick, or in prison, and not help You?"

Then He will answer them, "I assure you: Whatever you did not do for one of the least of these, you did not do for Me either."

And they will go away into eternal punishment, but the righteous into eternal life (Matthew 25:31-46).

You accuse us of being merely practitioners of the physical, and all that we accomplish with our hands is destined for death. But the objective of our work is not to change the world but to be obedient to the call of Jesus Christ—to love and repair broken people. Although that is an activity in the physical world, it is a spiritual discipline with heavenly implications.

THE PREACHERS, HAVING THE LAST WORD

Brothers and sisters, we cannot speak against what you feel called to do, but there are some simple facts that must be faced. We've overheard you talking, and we know about your plans to make disciples and plant churches through your schools and clinics. Yet, that doesn't seem to work anymore, at least not in those places as yet unreached with the Gospel. Muslims, Hindus, and Buddhists know about the proselytizing agenda of mission institutions, and they do not allow them to fulfill the objective of making disciples.

We can show you institutions all across Asia that have consumed millions of missionary dollars and have produced very little fruit for the Gospel. Commonly, mission hospitals in Muslim lands have worked for 50 years and do not have a viable church to show for it. Take a look at this example from *Revolution in World Missions* by K.P. Yohannan:

In few countries is the failure of Christian humanism more apparent than in Thailand. There, after 150 years of showing marvelous social compassion, the Church still makes up only one-tenth of 1 percent of the entire population.

Self-sacrificing missionaries probably have done more to modernize the country than any other single force. They gave the country the core of its civil service, education, and medical systems. Working closely with the royal family, the missionaries played the crucial role in eliminating slavery and keeping the country free of Western control during the colonial era.

Thailand owes to missionaries its widespread literacy, first printing press, first university, first hospital, first doctor, and almost every other benefit of education and science. In every area, including trade and diplomacy, Christian missionaries put the needs of the host nation first and helped usher in the twentieth century.

But today, virtually all that remains of this is a shell of good works. Millions have meanwhile slipped into eternity without the Lord. They died more educated, better governed, and healthier—but they died without Christ and are bound for hell.[2]

These social services do some marvelous things, but they do not bring us closer to establishing a healthy church. They do not obey the command of Jesus to go and make disciples of all nations.

MY THOUGHTS

God love them. I told you they were passionate. Frankly, I can find nothing wrong with the arguments on either side. We have just scratched the surface of this issue, and there are innumerable, if not particularly congenial, opinions among the many apostolic organizations. If you are particularly interested and want to have some fun, try to get into the head of each of the camps for a while. You can begin by doing an internet search on something like "value of preaching." The thousands of articles that extol the virtue of this work are enlightening. It seems that preachers can preach about anything, including the reason for preachin'. I particularly appreciated the article that stated, "The man that has the heavenly, holy, and high calling would almost rather preach than eat." Additionally, I laughed at the British preacher who was proud to point out that one really cannot find good preaching in an American pulpit.[3]

Our engagement tactics are largely born out of our bias; preachers engaging with preaching tactics and healers engaging with healing tactics.

Understanding the healers is a bit more difficult. There are over a half million hits on "Google" just for "medical mission," many of which describe a particular ministry. The point of all of this is that there are two camps of ministers. Both are called of God, both are skilled and passionate, but each approach the work from a different perspective. They may be able to agree on a common vision of establishing a multiplying national church, but, particularly if they live in a land of physically needy people, these two camps will diverge over tactics related to engagement. The preaching camp is biased toward tactics that involve preaching, and the healing camp is biased toward tactics that meet physical needs.

I cannot knock a hole in either argument. Both camps have enough scriptural firepower to put up a sustained fight. The question is whether these two camps are meant to work in this parallel tension or whether there is another option.

CHAPTER 2

ONE COMMAND

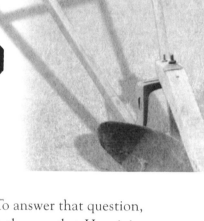

Was Jesus a *preacher* or was He a *healer?* To answer that question, one only needs to take a superficial look at the way that He ministered. He was able to maintain a perfect balance between preaching and healing. He demonstrated no bias toward either camp.

A great example of Jesus showing equal zeal for the ministries of preaching and healing is found in Luke:

> While the sun was setting, all those who had any who were sick with various diseases brought them to Him; and laying His hands on each one of them, *He was healing them.*
>
> When day came, Jesus left and went to a secluded place; and the crowds were searching for Him, and came to Him and tried to keep Him from going away from them.
>
> But He said to them, "*I must preach* the kingdom of God to the other cities also, for I was sent for this purpose" (Luke 4:40, 42-43, NASB; italics mine).

Jesus did not show a preference for one ministry over the other. He spent a day in healing and moved on to other towns to preach also. Think about it. Can you think of any example where Jesus complained about too many sick people getting in the way of His preaching or too many learners getting in the way of His healing ministry?

On the contrary, we only find that He preached and healed everywhere that He went: "Then Jesus went to all the towns and villages, teaching in their synagogues, *preaching* the good news of the kingdom, and *healing* every disease and every sickness" (Matthew 9:35).

The problem with this argument, though, is the same problem that we encounter with any argument in which we try to relate the behavior of Jesus to that of humankind. We don't have a divine nature. Rather than seeing issues through God's eyes, we filter everything the way sunglasses filter sunlight. A preacher, trained in preaching and with years of preaching experience, sees the world through that filter and will not naturally take to healing. At the same time, a healer who is schooled in healing or social services, and who has never preached, will have a difficult time seeing himself in a preaching capacity. People come with a bias.

At this point, I would ask that the reader put the entire matter of bias aside and further investigate the biblical teaching about preaching and healing. Before asking whether it is manageable or practical, let us see whether or not it is right.

Although we cannot hope to replicate the behavior of Jesus, He did encourage us to emulate His behavior. He did more than train through modeling and encouragement. He also gave instructions related to the subject in question. In fact, He had some very specific things to say on the subject. Every time that Jesus sent out disciples, He commanded them to benefit the needy *as* they preached the Gospel.

> And as you go, *preach*, saying, 'The kingdom of heaven is at hand.' *Heal* the sick, raise the dead, cleanse the lepers, cast out demons (Matthew 10:7-8, NASB; italics mine).

> And He summoned the twelve and began to send them out in pairs... They went out and *preached* that men should repent. And they were casting out many demons and were anointing with oil many sick people and *healing* them (Mark 6:7, 12-13, NASB; italics mine).

He sent them to *preach* the kingdom of God and to *heal* the sick (Luke 9:2, NKJV; italics mine).

After this, the Lord appointed 70 others, and He sent them ahead of Him in pairs to every town and place where He Himself was about to go.... "*Heal* the sick who are there, and *tell them*, 'The kingdom of God has come near you'" (Luke 10:1, 9; italics mine).

When we look at the book of Acts, we find that the disciples of Jesus, after His ascension into heaven, obeyed their Master and continued the "preach *and* heal" tradition seamlessly.

Jesus modeled the *preach and heal* tactic, He commanded it, and His disciples obeyed Him by using it as they went out.

Jesus commanded the apostles to remain in Jerusalem until they received the power of the Holy Spirit. This occurred on the day of Pentecost. On that day, through a movement of God's Spirit, 3,000 people became disciples of Jesus Christ, and we are told that this new church "devoted themselves to the apostles' *teaching*" (Acts 2:42; italics mine).

The very first story after the day of Pentecost, however, shifts straight into *healing*. In the same way that Jesus seemed to be incapable of walking past people who made requests of him, Peter and John, on their way to the temple, stopped at the request of a disabled beggar. Despite their intended agenda, they instinctively diverted their attention to this man.

Please indulge a short foray into this story as there are huge implications here. As you will see in a moment, the ability of Peter and John to alter their itinerary from the temple to this needy man resulted in the preaching of the Gospel before the entire Sanhedrin. I'm sure that Peter and John were guided to some degree by Jesus' instruction to "give to the one who asks you" (Matthew 5:42).

Although you will notice that Jesus did not say that one must necessarily give what is asked. In this story, Peter does not give the crippled man the money that he requested. Yet, they do not pass him by, as most of us would, because they had a different attitude toward beggars.

In most situations, when someone speaks to you, you will stop and answer them. Even if a stranger asks you the time of day, you will respond in some manner. The exception to this rule is beggars. When a beggar speaks, it is common for most of us to ignore him and keep walking. If we do speak, it is brief and from a distance.

Beggars, street people, and rag pickers wander the margins of society and are pushed to the periphery of our minds. We are intimidated by these people for a variety of reasons. An encounter with them is unpredictable, and deep down we fear it could result in embarrassment, violence, or some form of loss. And while we are *deep down*, could it be that we really consider these people as less than human, and that is why we do not consider them at all? The truth is that the value of any given beggar according to God's standard is equal to that of you, me, or any president or king.

The behavior of Peter and John, in perfect imitation of Jesus, is provocative on several levels. As they were going up to pray, a man who was crippled from birth asked them for money. Stating that he had no money to give, Peter took the man by the hand and with the words "In the name of Jesus Christ the Nazarene, get up and walk!" (Acts 3:6b) helped him to his feet. "At once his feet and ankles became strong. So he jumped up, stood, and started to walk, and he entered the temple complex with them—walking, leaping, and praising God" (Acts 3:7a-8).

Perhaps Peter and John saw the beggar through the eyes of the Holy Spirit, who was within them. If they had looked at the beggar with fleshly eyes, they certainly would have walked past. They may have considered tossing him a coin, but they wouldn't have come to a complete stop, putting on hold the pursuit of their own agenda to engage this interruption. On the other hand, they may have simply stopped because they had adopted the mind of Christ and had been transformed in their behavior; stopping for a beggar was perfectly natural.

We do not really know their motivation for stopping, but we do see that, after stopping, they again behaved like Jesus. The man asked for money, but Peter and John looked beyond that request to what the man really needed. Perhaps they remembered what they had been commanded to do: preach and heal.

As is common throughout the Gospels and the book of Acts, the healing of this man caused a large crowd to gather around Peter and John. At that point, Peter wasted no time in fulfilling the other half of the one command to *preach and heal*. "Men of Israel, why are you amazed at this? Or why do you stare at us, as though by our own power or godliness we had made him walk? The God of Abraham, Isaac, and Jacob, the God of our fathers, has glorified His Servant Jesus" (Acts 3:12-13).

It took Peter only three sentences to take the focus off of the healing and put it on Jesus. From that point, he *preached* to the crowd and made this appeal: "Therefore repent and turn back, that your sins may be wiped out so that seasons of refreshing may come from the presence of the Lord, and He may send Jesus, who has been appointed Messiah for you" (Acts 3:19-20).

Acts 4:4 tells us that many who heard the message believed, and the number of disciples grew to about 5,000. We have no evidence that this great sermon was planned. We also do not have any evidence that Peter or John heard a voice from the Holy Spirit telling them that this disabled man would be a pathway to a great preaching opportunity. But we do have evidence that they obeyed the command of Jesus to go, preach, and heal. The results were growth of the kingdom and glory to God. And this event wasn't the only preaching opportunity that came from the healing.

Because the content of the sermon was disturbing to the religious leaders, Peter and John were arrested and held overnight. The next day they were brought to appear before the high priest, rulers, elders, teachers, and many influential leaders. On this occasion, Peter began telling his audience about Jesus with his first sentence: "If we are being examined today about a good deed done to a disabled man—by what means he was healed—let it be known to all of you and to the people of Israel, that by the name of Jesus Christ the Nazarene—whom you crucified and whom God raised from the dead—by Him this man is standing here before you healthy" (Acts 4:9-10).

This is just one example of how the apostles obeyed Jesus' command to preach and heal. Just a few verses later, we are told: "And with great power the apostles were giving testimony to the resurrection of the Lord Jesus, and great grace was on all of them. For there was not a needy person among them, because all those who owned lands or houses sold them, brought the proceeds of the things that were sold, and laid them at the apostles' feet. This was then distributed to each person as anyone had a need" (Acts 4:33-35).

Here we see preaching as testifying to the resurrection of the Lord Jesus. Healing, in this case, met the needs of all the people. The preach and heal tradition continues into chapter five where we see yet another example: "A multitude came together from the towns surrounding Jerusalem, bringing sick people and those who were tormented by unclean spirits, and they were all healed" (Acts 5:16).

As in the first story, these healings resulted in trouble. Instead of two apostles being arrested and giving testimony before the Sanhedrin, all of the apostles were arrested. When told not to preach anymore in the name of Jesus, Peter and the other apostles replied, "We must obey God rather than men. The God of our fathers raised up Jesus, whom you had murdered by hanging Him on a tree. God exalted this man to His right hand as ruler and Savior, to grant repentance to Israel, and forgiveness of sins. We are witnesses of these things, and so is the Holy Spirit whom God has given to those who obey Him" (Acts 5:29-32).

It is not difficult to see that Jesus' practice of preaching and healing became the standard practice of the disciples immediately after His ascension into heaven. Interestingly, the juxtaposition of preaching and healing was not necessarily scheduled, but rather the one was precipitated by the other. Like Jesus, disciples naturally tended to the needs of hurting people, which provided more opportunities to preach the Gospel, even among the rulers of the area.

Jesus sent out all of His disciples to preach and to heal. They were given one command, because the two ministries work together in God's master strategy. The New Testament reveals many examples of how the apostles continued with this tactic, resulting in growth of the church and glory to God. Whether it is natural or easy, we see that this methodology simply is right. Jesus did not send some out to preach and some out to heal. But as we have become more specialized, that is what most apostolic ministers today are doing. We have separated these two ministries so that healing ministries are done by healers and preaching ministries are done by preachers.

We put the issue of bias aside for a time, but now let's look at that bias and investigate why we have separated preaching from healing. And let us find out if it is possible to put them back together again.

CHAPTER 3

WE GO WITH WHAT WE KNOW

Medical education is hard. Medical education is long. Medical education is expensive. Once it is complete, however, there is great satisfaction in being a doctor. I have to admit that it comes with automatic status, prestige, and a title which indicates that the bearer, by some mysterious and poorly understood virtue by non-doctors, is someone who can be trusted with even the most intimate of problems.

I'll probably get kicked out of the doctor club for revealing this, but long ago doctors got together and created a doctor subculture with secret handshakes and code words. The purpose was to build a mystique around the practice of medicine so that it would be elevated, in the minds of non-doctors, to some greater-than-ordinary-man status. The facade is maintained through the use of many fancy words and cryptic writings, but the ultimate piece of the plan that makes it work is the magic title of "doctor."

I so enjoy the title of "doctor" that I have determined to share it with everyone that I know. I call both of my children "doctor," our cats are both doctors, my wife is an honorary doctor, and I call all of my friends "doctor." The way I see it, it's a fun title that everyone should enjoy.

For someone who finally has achieved the goal of being a real doctor, however, personal identity can become completely entwined with identity as a doctor. It is no joking matter to many. From the moment we step into medical school, we are brainwashed to believe that the practice of medicine is more sacred than any other profession. The divorce rates are high among physicians because they frequently prioritize identity as physician high above identity as spouse or parent.

Lest you wag your head in pity over us, just think of some of the preachers that you know. My time in seminary has shown me that preachers have no less of a subculture. They are also highly trained and specialized. They take years to earn a master's degree or a doctorate, and as with doctors, their personal identity becomes entwined in that title of priest, preacher, pastor, minister, or evangelist. Congregations or admirers elevate preachers to demigod status, and they work tirelessly to maintain that position. There are also rumors that they sometimes neglect their spouses and children because "the ministry demands it" in much the same way as doctors.

It is certain that God is calling both healers and preachers to His mission field, and naturally these individuals come with their own identities. But we can see one factor that has greatly contributed to the separation of the preaching and healing ministries is the emphasis on academic achievement and specialization prior to one being commissioned as an apostolic minister. When Jesus was calling young fishermen right off the beach, He was able to mold their identities into preacher-healers. Because apostolic ministers today show up with so much academic background, our starting point is much more compartmentalized.

A farmer with a college degree in agriculture, who comes to the mission field as an agriculturist, sees himself in that *compartment*. In his home country, he identifies himself as a farmer. When he arrives on the mission field, he sees himself no differently, although his dual identity is now a "missionary farmer." He does the things he is trained to do. He farms, he teaches farming, and he involves himself in farming projects. When he gets hungry, he sits at the lunch table with the healers because of commonalities. He brings healing to hurting people through better nutrition.

A seminary graduate will identify himself as a priest, preacher, minister, or pastor. On the mission field he will do the things that he was trained in seminary to do. He will look for opportunities to preach, whether it's to a large audience, a family, or somebody in a coffee shop. He has a brain full of theological knowledge that is brimming over and must be poured out on somebody. When he stops for a break, he will sit at the lunch table with other preachers because his identity is in preaching.

Just as an aside, when a mother brings in a sick child, it is not uncommon for her to tell the physician that the child has stopped eating solid food and only wants to breastfeed. Or perhaps he has stopped walking and will only crawl. Individuals under stress revert back to that with which they are most comfortable. If they have recently ventured out into a new arena, they abandon that lesser-known territory for better-known ground when they are sick, afraid, or otherwise stressed. The mission field is the greatest of stressors where the natural thing is for people to stick close to that with which they are most familiar. The farmer on the mission field is even more likely to stick close to farming, and the preacher is even more likely to stick close to preaching.

If you have not been to medical school, you cannot know the surreal feeling of walking as a group of intimidated, first-year medical students into a large, cold laboratory containing 40 human cadavers wrapped in clear plastic. The first day of human anatomy class is not comfortable for any student. Every medical student stretches himself as the body is unwrapped, turned over, and dissected. It is a difficult and unnatural experience in the beginning, but within weeks it is all done without thought.

Forcing ourselves to do something we consider unnatural is not common. In general, we play very close to the house. We do those things that we are comfortable doing. In a highly specialized culture, this means that we do those things that we are particularly trained to do. Unless they are somehow pushed out, the farmer and the seminary graduate will ordinarily stay within their comfort zones. Decades will pass with them doing the same type of ministry and sitting at the same lunch tables. So, what makes one begin a new behavior that is right, but is seemingly as unnatural as beginning dissection on a cadaver?

Darley and Batson's "Good Samaritan Study" of 1973 has become rather famous with preachers. In the study, a number of Princeton seminary students were asked to give a talk at a recording studio. Half of the students were given the topic of the Good Samaritan, and half were given another topic. Half of the students were told that they were late, and half were told that they had some time to spare. Along the route, Darley and Batson had positioned an actor, slumped in a doorway, coughing and groaning in pain.

The results of the study were that only 10 percent of hurried students stopped to help the needy man. Interestingly, whether or not the student was on his way to speak on the topic of the Good Samaritan or another topic made no statistical difference in the outcome of the study. When you're in a hurry, it doesn't matter what's on your mind; you ain't stoppin'. Sadly, though, only about 60 percent of students stopped even when they weren't in a hurry.[4]

Hurried people don't stop, and that point is well made. But I think there is a second point here. Keeping in mind that these are seminary students, I am surprised that only about 60 percent stopped to help someone in need, even though they were told that they had time to spare. How could 40 percent of these men or women of God be so callous in the face of someone in need? And remember the percentage of non-helpers was 90 percent when they were in a hurry.

In my opinion, the answer is directly related to this issue of identity compartmentalization. Western people especially see themselves within the compartment of a certain identity to such a degree that they can relinquish responsibility to issues they interpret as being outside of their compartment. In other words, if they don't see it as fitting into their box, they feel like it is someone else's responsibility. These students, then, see the person in need and quickly rationalize, "What do I know about coughing and pain? I'm a seminarian. Someone else will be better at taking care of this than I." This thought frees the young student to keep walking. After all, if it had been an issue related to a "preaching emergency," the student probably would have stopped and engaged.

This world is so specialized that I refer a patient who has injured a hand to a physician who was once a surgeon, became a plastic surgeon, and did extra training to become a hand specialist. I suggest that, in the same way, each of us has a compartmental identity, be it engineer, homemaker, preacher, or healer, which is mostly defined by training and experience. We have a level of comfort surrounding things related to this identity, and we look to unidentified others to pick up the slack for all those things that we think we can't do.

As another example, rarely does anyone feel like the Great Commission was directed at him or her. One thinks, "My name isn't on that list of disciples. Those guys were like Jedi Masters. I'd get creamed if I tried to go out there and do what they did." But we do think that there is someone else out there, somewhere, who *is* qualified to do those things that we consider remarkable.

The psychological phenomenon of identity compartmentalization has come about because of the current societal emphasis on academic achievement and specialization. This emphasis is obviously true and probably necessary in areas such as engineering and medicine, but is it necessary in the church? Average pew sitters sit in a building designed by a professional architect, hear music by professional musicians, hear a sermon from a professional teacher, and have their children taught by professional youth workers. If someone tried to practice medicine without a license, it would be illegal, but do you see how we are sending the message that the same thing applies to the practice of Christianity? According to our current model, it is only appropriate for religious activities to be performed by those who are trained and paid for those activities. Since many of us have no training or background in these things, they are outside of our compartmental identity, and we see ourselves as relieved from participation.

When my wife and I first arrived in South Asia, we were told that our real job was church planting. "What?" I thought. "I have no idea how to start a church." My head swam with images of the kind of church that I just described. How can we afford a building and all of that equipment? And how can we train a pastor in a country like this? The model of church I knew had professionals do all of the work, and that's the only kind of church I could envision. Actually, I had no idea what Christ's *church* really was.

Since it was my job, though, I started studying the Bible and quickly found out how simple it all should be. I didn't need a building, sound equipment, a seminary-trained pastor, or even an organ. All I needed was disciples, and with the Lord's help I could make those. According to the biblical model, no professional training is necessary for any position in the church. Overseers, teachers, and the spiritually gifted were just disciples of Jesus, like all of us who are born again. Like all authentic disciples, they performed services as the Holy Spirit enabled them—not within those realms for which they had been schooled. The professionalism and specialization that so dominate our current church model are extra-biblical.

As our engagement tactics are largely born out of our bias, our bias is largely born out of our educational background.

Remember the poignant story of Peter and John going up to the temple to pray? Because they saw themselves as disciples of Jesus—people with no agenda of their own—they immediately stopped at the request of a disabled beggar. This interruption resulted in the preaching of the Gospel to many and significant growth of the church.

If you see yourself as a healer, you will limit yourself to that sphere. If your identity is in preaching, then you limit yourself to that. Both mistakes will cut you off from using the master plan of "preach and heal" that Jesus has laid out for all whose identity is simply that of "disciple."

Beside Barnabas the encourager, my hero is Dr. Luke. He's got that neat title of "doctor," but that's just the beginning of his greatness. He is obviously the greatest medical apostle who ever lived.

Dr. Luke wrote the books of Luke and Acts—more of the New Testament than any other writer. The book of Luke pays more attention to Jesus' concern for women, Gentiles, and the marginalized people of society than the other Gospels. In addition, this book is a full account of the life of Jesus. It provides the details of the incarnation of God in Jesus all the way through His atoning sacrifice on the cross, resurrection from the grave, and ascension into heaven.

The book of Acts is the only account that we have of the coming of the Holy Spirit at Pentecost and the struggles of the apostles as they faced a lost world without Jesus. It describes the birth of the early church and how God continued to work in power through His agents to spread the Gospel to the nations, even in the absence of the Christ.

How could we fulfill our apostolic task without the book of Acts to teach and encourage us? And how many people have come to faith from reading the book of Luke or by seeing the *JESUS* film, which is based on that book? Perhaps Dr. Luke's work is responsible for more people coming into the kingdom of heaven than any other single person.

If Dr. Luke is the greatest medical apostle, what is it about him that we should emulate? Was he a skilled medical practitioner? Was he devoted to his patients and medical or surgical practice? Perhaps he was a famous preacher? Obviously, we have no record that this was the case.

What a paradox. The man who may have had the greatest impact for the kingdom of God has not done it through preaching nor through healing, but through writing. As far as we know, Dr. Luke never preached at all. We have no indication that he even continued to practice medicine. On the contrary, and this is vital, when he became a disciple of Jesus, he humbled himself and abandoned what he loved most. He obediently became a writer so that the books of Luke and Acts might be recorded, through the inspiration of the Holy Spirit, for billions to read. Although he was trained as a healer, he really made his impact when he completely lost that identity. His identity became simply *a disciple of Jesus Christ*.

Dr. Luke is a hero because of his character. He sacrificed everything (surgery, delivering babies, and writing prescriptions) to obey the call on his life. He did not try to find a way to fit the two together, because they were incompatible. The character and the discipline of Luke just described are completely abnormal and unnatural—and that is the key to this conundrum.

What I mean is this. As a doctor, the *natural* thing would have been for Dr. Luke to have remained a doctor and to have followed Paul and the other preachers around doing doctoring things. But Luke didn't put any preconditions or parameters on his call from God. He did not say, "I will go anywhere or do anything as long as it relates to being a doctor." On the contrary, Dr. Luke is one of the best examples of a man who completely crucified his identify for Jesus Christ and let the Holy Spirit direct him. Look what happened. God used the combination of his education and his great compassion to make him one of the most important writers of all time.

Think of how many parables Jesus told about servants. He thinks of us in this manner, so why do we think so differently of ourselves? A good servant is not an opinionated servant, but quietly obedient. This perceived identity, as a servant or as a true disciple such as Luke, is the answer to the question that was asked earlier: What makes one begin a new behavior that is right, but is seemingly as unnatural as beginning dissection on a cadaver? It may not be natural, easy, or comfortable, but those objections are irrelevant. It was commanded by our Lord, so it must be done. And when we see ourselves as His servants, we obey instinctively.

Thus, if a trained seminarian sees someone who is coughing and in pain, and his identity is as a servant of Jesus Christ, he will stop to help. In the same way, if this disciple is only a theologically ignorant doctor, and a crowd gathers because of the healing services being provided, the Gospel will proceed from him boldly. Healers must also preach, and preachers must also heal. Our personal bias or training is irrelevant and must not be allowed to become an idol. Jesus gave all of us the strategic tactic to "preach and heal" so that we may grip the lost through the power of the Holy Spirit, that disciples may be made of all nations, and that the knowledge of the glory of the Lord may cover the earth as the waters cover the seas.

The preach and heal strategy is a two-handled plow.

I am not saying that these two ministries have equal importance. Rather, I am saying that the question as to which ministry is more important is the wrong question to ask. Those who uphold the value of preaching *or* healing are focusing on mere activities rather than on the glorious kingdom. It doesn't matter which ministry is more important. What matters is obedience to the directives of Jesus. He is the master strategist. He knows what He is doing and has given us this tactic as a two-handled plow. Both handles must be held with equal pressure and commitment for the one plow blade to dig deep into the ground and transform the soil into a place best prepared for the seed. If priority is given to one handle or the other, the furrow will go off at an angle and spoil the field. But if each handle is grasped firmly, and the worker does not look back, the plow will work as it was intended. When bias and preference have been crucified, and the preach and heal method is driven straight forward by the force of the Holy Spirit, God is able to plant the seed of His Gospel into the hearts of people.

It is possible to choose either tactic of preaching or healing to make progress with disciple making. But that progress is sure to be much slower, because there will not be the synergy that comes from using these two tactics together. Rather than using an efficient two-handled plow, which digs deep with ease, one would be digging furrows with a one-handled tool, such as a hoe. A hoe is much less efficient and requires more dependence on the one handling the tool.

CHAPTER 4

IS STRATEGY A BAD WORD?

In Acts 15, Paul and Barnabas, apostolic partners, go separate ways. The Holy Spirit inspired Dr. Luke to follow and record the work of Paul, but what of Barnabas? We have no record of his travels or church-planting work. Was it any less successful than Paul's? What did the other apostles do after the ascension of Jesus? Did they live quiet lives in Jerusalem or Galilee? Or did they also travel and make disciples?

For some reason, God has decided to keep these other works archived and hidden from our generation, and, like me, many of you are hoping that there is a DVD vault in heaven where we can find out what happened to our heroes. Barnabas has always been my main man, but I have also been curious about Thomas in India. How did he get there, and how did he communicate?

Until we get to heaven, we have church tradition that at least indicates that Paul was not the only apostle to travel and plant churches extensively. These traditions are not biblical, but here is a brief look at what they tell us:

John Mark: In addition to traveling with Paul and Barnabas, he traveled across Northern Africa into Egypt and Libya. It is believed that he was also with Peter in Rome and acted as his translator. Tradition tells us that he was martyred in Alexandria.

Peter: The New Testament does tell us that he preached in Samaria, Lydda, Joppa, Caesarea, Jerusalem, Corinth, Antioch, and Babylon. He also traveled to Rome where he was martyred.

Andrew: It is believed that Andrew preached to the Scythians, in modern day Georgia, as far as the Caspian Sea. He also went to Istanbul and from there to Greece where he was martyred by crucifixion.

John, son of Zebedee: He visited Rome and Asia Minor and spent many years in Ephesus, Turkey. He was exiled to Patmos, but may have been released in his old age, and died in Ephesus around 100 AD.

Phillip: He traveled with Bartholomew into Asia Minor. He possibly visited France as well.

Bartholomew: Most likely he visited Asia Minor with Phillip. He was also reported to have visited Armenia with Jude and Azerbaijan where he was martyred.

Thomas: There is much tradition to connect Thomas to preaching in many parts of India, and he was also said to have preached in Iraq, Iran, and China.

Matthew or Levi: He stayed in Palestine for 15 years and then traveled to Persian Ethiopia, Macedonia, Syria, and African Ethiopia.

Jude Thaddaeus: He was one of the first apostles to leave Jerusalem. He traveled to Armenia with Bartholomew and Thomas and died in Syrian Persia.

Simon the Canaanite (Zealot): He traveled to Egypt and across Northern Africa to Carthage. He fled Rome after the Claudian Edict and arrived in Britain in 44 AD. He also traveled through Palestine, Syria, and Mesopotamia and was martyred in Persia with Jude.

Matthias: He traveled to Armenia and may have also worked alongside Andrew.[5]

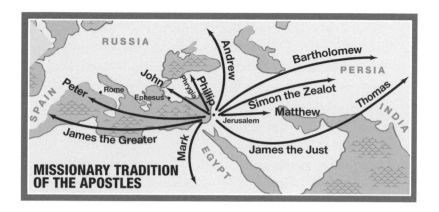

RUSSIA

Andrew

Bartholomew

PERSIA

John

Peter

Rome

Phrygia

Phillip

Thomas

Ephesus

SPAIN

Simon the Zealot

Matthew

INDIA

Jerusalem

James the Greater

Mark

James the Just

EGYPT

MISSIONARY TRADITION OF THE APOSTLES

One cannot say why the majority of New Testament apostolic exploits are Pauline, but one also cannot deny that they are. According to tradition, all of the apostles advanced the Gospel into unreached places as a means to establish the church. God could have easily given us the exciting stories of Andrew in Russia, Thomas in India, or Matthew in Africa, but He did not. For now, through the book of Acts and the Pauline Epistles, God has primarily given us the stories of Paul's struggles and victories as he took the Gospel into Turkey and Greece. That fact alone makes these stories worthy of our attention.

A present day reader easily can see how Jesus' command to make disciples of all nations was lived out by one of the earliest apostles. Paul and his companions were driven forward by the Holy Spirit despite the dangers, establishing local churches and spreading the Gospel throughout entire regions.

Paul's first apostolic journey:

At Pisidian Antioch: "When the Gentiles heard this, they rejoiced and glorified the message of the Lord, and all who had been appointed to eternal life believed. So *the message of the Lord spread through the whole region*... And the disciples were filled with joy and the Holy Spirit" (Acts 13:48-49, 52; italics mine).

At Iconium: "The same thing happened in Iconium; they entered the Jewish synagogue and spoke in such *a way that a great number of both Jews and Greeks believed.* But the Jews who refused to believe stirred up and poisoned the minds of the Gentiles against the brothers. So they stayed there for some time and spoke boldly, in reliance on the Lord, who testified to the message of His grace by granting that signs and wonders be performed through them. But the people of the city were divided, some siding with the Jews and some with the apostles" (Acts 14:1-4; italics mine).

At Derbe: "… they had evangelized that town and *made many disciples*" (Acts 14:21a; italics mine).

Second apostolic journey:
At Corinth: "So he left there and went to the house of a man named Titius Justus, a worshiper of God, whose house was next door to the synagogue. Crispus, the leader of the synagogue, believed the Lord, along with his whole household; and *many of the Corinthians, when they heard, believed and were baptized.*

Then the Lord said to Paul in a night vision, 'Don't be afraid, but keep on speaking and don't be silent. For I am with you, and no one will lay a hand on you to hurt you, *because I have many people in this city*'" (Acts 18:7-10; italics mine).

Third apostolic journey:
At Ephesus: "He [Paul] withdrew from them and met separately with the disciples, conducting discussions every day in the lecture hall of Tyrannus. And this went on for two years, *so that all the inhabitants of the province of Asia, both Jews and Greeks, heard the word of the Lord.* God was

performing extraordinary miracles by Paul's hands... In this way *the Lord's message flourished* and prevailed" (Acts 19:9b-11, 20; italics mine).

Paul worked for about 15 years. A typical term for contemporary apostolic workers is usually four years overseas with one year in the home country. So Paul worked the equivalent of three modern-day apostolic terms. During that time he visited cities across a distance of about 1,000 miles and established churches in at least eight different cities. As the italicized verses indicate, we also know that these churches multiplied so that the Gospel spread throughout all of Turkey and Greece. Whatever Paul was doing worked. Since God has chosen to preserve mainly these Pauline accounts and the epistles that accompany them, it is only fitting that we look closely at the strategy of this team and learn from the very method that God chose to pass on to us.

This book is not primarily about church planting. One can develop techniques of evangelism, disciple making, and church formation based upon study of Scripture, one's spiritual gifts, and the context of ministry. However, there are a few general principles to observe from Paul's strategy. Before getting into that, though, let us ask the question of how far we should go with strategy building.

Isn't the world often categorized into two kinds of people? One can be a cat or dog person, night or morning person, beach or mountain person. And I just told you about preachers or healers. Well, we also have "strategy lovers" and "strategy leavers."

Many people object to the energy that is put into strategy building. They feel that it places too much emphasis on man's work rather than on trusting God. After all, a key principle in Acts is that they were led by the Holy Spirit.

Obviously, I would never argue against this point. If we are to have any success in the business of making disciples, it will be as a result of divine intervention. Are any of us clever enough to talk another human being into this new way of life, especially when it could result in imprisonment or death? No. Disciple making is characterized by divine help and power. God uses our work, but it's He who builds the kingdom.

Those who emphasize reliance on the power and guidance of the Holy Spirit are right. It is always our prayer and expectation that our projects and programs will be hijacked by God and driven in His direction. The purpose of this book is to bring His apostolic ministers and the people of unreached nations together, positioning them so that there is something for God to hijack.

We can't predict or control what God will do. But by positioning apostolic ministers and the peoples of unreached nations together, we do provide a venue for God to do something great!

Strategy is not a bad word, but church-planting strategy certainly does not indicate a detailed plan that automatically will result in the making of disciples and churches. That is the strategy objective and our hope. That is our vision when we pray. But the making of disciples and church establishment are the work of God, not men. So strategy development is simply a starting place that identifies where we are, where God says to go, and how to make intentional steps forward, trusting Him for all progress and everything that we need. It is a means to best position ourselves so that, as in the biblical examples, God can work through us to accomplish His purpose.

We know that if we stay in our homes and watch television, no disciples will be made. Yet, if we enter into the homes of nationals, lay our hands on the sick, and preach the Gospel, God can do something amazing. Perhaps, as in the story of Peter and John at the temple, the Gospel will spread throughout the whole city.

After I get to heaven and watch the DVDs of the apostles, I look forward to seeing those of the apostolic workers who followed them. Sadly, only a little was written for over a millennium, and we have only vague hints as to how the Gospel advanced after Dr. Luke's book. In Acts 19:20, we learned *"the Lord's message flourished and prevailed*," but we don't really know to what degree. A brief look at history seems to reveal that God has worked off and on in this way since the day of Pentecost. There are many stories of amazing disciple movements, and there also seem to be centuries of stagnation. One cannot deny, however, that the Gospel has spread remarkably from the day of Pentecost to this present time. Sixty percent of the earth's population is currently reached with the Gospel.

INTRODUCING YEAST

I suppose all apostolic workers imagine their dreams coming true. We all lay awake at night and envision the Gospel spreading from community to community where we work. In these dreams, the Lord works with great power, the forces of darkness are vanquished, every family in our region has access to the Gospel, huge numbers of disciples are made, churches are established everywhere, and great glory is given to God. We know that our God is the same as that of the apostolic fathers, and we are just looking for the same kinds of miracles and results that they saw. Indeed, great movements of the church have occurred around the world throughout history and are going on right now among many peoples.

About 50 years ago, Missiologist Donald A. MacGavran noted movements of the Gospel in his book *The Bridges of God*. He coined the term "people movements" and related stories occurring in Burma (Myanmar), Pakistan, Indonesia, India, Africa, and the Islands of the Pacific. Some of these movements resulted in more than 1 million people claiming the label of "Christian" just decades after the beginning of apostolic work. He emphasized that these were not just nominal believers, but ordinarily were healthy congregations of disciples.

He wrote:

> They [people movements] have provided over 90 percent of the growth of the newer churches throughout the world... One of the curious facts about people movements is that they have seldom been sought or desired... One wonders what would have happened had missions from

the beginning of the "Great Century" [1800 to 1914] been actively searching and praying for the coming of Christ-ward marches by the various peoples making up the population of the world.[6]

MacGavran observed that, despite the absence of intentionality, the Gospel was often passed from family to family and community to community until it had marched across an entire land. Isn't this reminiscent of *the message of the Lord spread through the whole region and all the inhabitants of the province of Asia, both Jews and Greeks, heard the word of the Lord?*

Because disciple making of entire ethnic peoples rather than individuals was prevalent, MacGavran proposed that it was attainable. In fact, he maintained that we should correctly adjust our strategy so that people movements become our stated objective. Scripture indicates that it was Paul's objective. Shouldn't it be our objective as well? As MacGavran said, "Christward movements of peoples are the supreme goal of missionary effort."[7]

In 1989, at a global missionary meeting called Global Consultation on World Evangelism (GCOWE), a "Great Commission Manifesto" was written, stating that, among other ingredients, our strategy should be to "establish a mission-minded church-planting movement within every unreached people group so that the Gospel is accessible to all people."[8] The term "church-planting movement" is an evolution of MacGavran's term "people movement" but describes the same phenomenon.

These movements are a modern-day expression of the same Gospel movements that were seen in Acts. They describe the permeation of the Gospel throughout an ethnic or geographic region rather than the making of isolated disciples. Rather than additive, they indicate a *multiplicative* increase of disciples and churches. It is as Jesus taught: "... The kingdom of heaven is like yeast that a woman took and mixed into 50 pounds of flour until it spread through all of it" (Matthew 13:33).

It is important to note, however, that the multiplication of indigenous churches is our objective but is not our standard for success.

I have had several contributors to my apostolic education, but the greatest of these was a man named Ed. Ed and his wife, Barb, moved to a Muslim country in South Asia in 1956. I met them in their 39th year of service when my family arrived there in 1995. Ed told me how they had come to that country with three other families, and they had all dreamed of seeing "church-planting movements." Yet, in all of their years, they saw only handfuls come to Christ and no multiplying indigenous church ever formed. It was difficult for him to return to America to raise support, often speaking after a missionary to Brazil who had seen thousands come to Christ.

Ed convinced me that he and Barb were closely attuned to the voice of God and were faithfully living out their assignment. On one occasion, Ed and I took a trip into a restricted region. Ed taught me how to be friendly with border guards so that we could enter areas that were off limits. During our first day of driving, we stopped 14 times to have tea or drink a Coke with Ed's friends. I spent all of that night in the bathroom. During most of these stops, Ed either prayed for the family or shared the Gospel in the national language.

After more than 40 years of overseas service, Ed and Barb retired from their organization. Since disciples never retire from following the guidance of their Lord, they returned to the same house in South Asia. Their new assignment, according to Ed, was to pray and fast for the people of their beloved country until Jesus returned or called them home. Within the next year, Barb and then Ed died.

Is it conceivable that these apostolic ministers will appear before the Judgment Seat of Christ as failures? Could Jesus possibly say anything to them other than "Well done, good and faithful servants"? I credit Ed as the most successful man I have ever known. He was obedient to the Lord and was sound in his vision and methodology. But like many great apostolic ministers of the past, his and his wife's great deeds are nowhere recorded on this earth. Perhaps after they are forgotten, the day of salvation for the peoples among whom they worked will come. Ed and Barb planted and watered. It is certain that the Lord who directed their life's work will not forget the work invested, and *He* will cause the growth and send others to reap the harvest. The people of the earth may have forgotten the earlier workers, but both he who sowed and he who reaped will be rewarded for their labor (1 Corinthians 3:6-9).

Indigenous movements of disciples and churches are not our measure of success; only obedience is. Do not concern yourself with the thoughts of others. God is your only audience. You work for Him and will be judged according to your obedience or lack of obedience to His directions.

Our objective is indigenous movements of reproducing churches. We must pursue them with all intent. This is also what Ed dreamed of and worked toward.

Years after Ed and Barb had moved on to heaven, I was talking about them with a colleague who also had been influenced by Ed's teaching. We talked about the thousands of hours put in by those four families who had stayed in the country for 40 years. My friend said, "Ed used to look me straight in the eyes and beg me to please use and build on the things that they had learned."

"Don't you dare go out and start from scratch," Ed told him. "Stand on our shoulders so that you can reach higher for Christ."

I like the concept of church-planting movements and will be using the term. If one goes out as a servant of the Lord Jesus Christ to make disciples, to establish His church, and to teach that church to multiply, he is making an offering to the Lord. This is an offering that the Lord can take and "hijack" in His marvelous and sometimes dramatic way to do whatever He wants. Yes, it may be that this work will be the planting and watering stages which do not see a harvest. But there can be no harvest without the planting and watering. Because of the greatness of our God, one's work may very well result in an explosive multiplication of churches. He can do anything with any people group.

The first three chapters are dedicated to one point because it is vital that you get it. There are two disciplines to be embraced and expressed in the making of disciples. Remember the *preach and heal* story of Peter and John as they went up to the temple to pray? It was a perfect health strategy because they provided compassionate health services to a hurting individual, which resulted in preaching the Gospel. All of the strategies in the latter section of this book will have these two components. They will meet needs of hurting people, provide daily opportunities for preaching, and position the apostolic workers so that God can use His power to bring about a Christward movement.

My sincere hope is that you get this point. Sadly, billions of dollars are spent each year on health projects by disciples of Jesus in which the practitioners have no disciple-making agenda. At the same time, every day preachers walk by beggars or rag pickers and drive by refugee camps with millions of residents without ever really acknowledging these people as human or obeying Jesus' command to minister to the needy. Who knows how God could use either of the above situations if His disciples were intentionally preaching *and* healing?

PART TWO
The Incarnational Element

CHAPTER 5

INGREDIENTS, METHODS, AND PRODUCTS

"Are you a believer?" I whispered, not knowing if one had to keep that a secret in Singapore. I was riding on a bus and a girl wearing a cross necklace sat down beside me.

"Yes," she said excitedly. "Are you?"

"Yes, I am," I responded. I had been overseas for a few years, and it was always exciting for me to talk with an Asian disciple. I wondered what her religious beliefs had been prior to coming to Christ. Then I asked, "So, where do you go to church?"

She just looked at me strangely, with her head cocked to the side, and I wondered if she spoke English. When she didn't answer, I repeated the question.

"Where do you go to church?"

Again, she tilted her head and couldn't answer. We sat in awkward silence. I had no idea what I had said that was wrong. If she was a believer, she had to go to church someplace, didn't she? Or did she? What was a church? At the time, I was envisioning a red brick building with white columns out front and a sign that said, "First Something-or-Other Church, Sunday School, 9:30 –10:45, Worship, 11:00 –12:00."

About five minutes later, she said, "My church meets on Tuesday nights… Sometimes everyone comes to my house." And I realized that I still had a lot to learn.

Grasping the biblical concept of church is essential for proper strategy development. If you have some mistaken ideas about what your finished product will be like, you will make mistakes as you plan, gather resources, and build. Over the past two millennia in many places of the world, our practice of church has drifted greatly from the biblical description and sometimes from biblical imperatives. Perhaps modernization is responsible, but mostly it is due to natural human tendency to add, alter, pick, and choose from that which God has given us.

Besides the essentials of church, we have picked up many nonessentials over the centuries that have become standards. Only a few of these new "standards" are non-biblical; most are just extra-biblical. And anything extra can slow one down. The church described in Scripture is much simpler and the preferred model over the church of today, because it is more reliant on the Holy Spirit and is most conducive to multiplication.

Additions to the biblical church are only symptoms of a deeper problem. As is expressed in the opening illustration, there is commonly a complete misunderstanding about what the church is. When one thinks of the church as a place, such as a red brick building with white columns, it naturally follows that "we need to fix up the church." If it is a place, shouldn't it be well-maintained and desirous? Shouldn't it have the best of everything, including comfortable seating, the best acoustics, and convenient parking? It only took me about three years as an apostolic minister to understand that the church is not a place.

The other mistake most commonly made by Westerners is to think of church as an event. In my early years as a church planter, I used to make this mistake by asking our new disciples if or when they were "having church." Or we will frequently say, "It is eleven o'clock. It is time to start church." Or even worse, "I'll meet you after church is over." Just as church is not a place, neither is it an event. If you think of it as an event, the symptoms of that mistake will manifest themselves in the hiring of professional performers and the purchase of expensive production equipment. After all, we want our "church" to be something that will excite people, which would necessitate a full band, a great sound system, lights, choir, and a professional speaker. But look it up. Church is not an event.

We are the church. The church may gather at a certain place. That place may even be a building, although this greatly increases the likelihood that attendees will wander down the path of misunderstanding the nature of church. But in no way is it a place, whether a house, rented space, or designated building. In the same way, when disciples gather as a church, they naturally fellowship, pray, and learn from the Bible. But the stuff that they do together is not "church." *The disciples themselves are church.* Neither the church building nor the time of worship is the bride of Christ. We are the bride of Christ. He died for us, not for buildings or programs.

Imagine that the only boat you had ever seen was the Titanic, and you were tasked with building a boat. How would you feel? How many boats do you think you could build in a year? How much money would you need, and where would you get it?

But what if I showed you a raft made out of long, strong, local trees that were lashed together with vines and told you that this was also a boat. Now how do you feel about the task of building boats? Are you encouraged? Do you believe that you can build more of these in a year? Do you need money to build these?

This example is a little bit dangerous. When someone's tradition of doing things is threatened, criticism arises. Frankly, many people are in love with and defend their church buildings and church programs. In the analogy, we are saying that a boat is simply a floating water vessel. The Titanic and a raft both fit that definition, but the Titanic is weighed down with lots of extras. Do not take this analogy to mean that one should in any way compromise the definition or practice of the church to speed multiplication. On the contrary, I am saying that the original definition of church is much simpler than what has evolved. An understanding and practice of the original and biblical definition of church is vital so as to recapture the ease with which the Gospel moves throughout entire regions.

Slowly, the scales are beginning to fall from the eyes of more disciples around the world. Traditional models of church are being abandoned for the biblical and more replicable model. Honestly, the best church I have ever met with was less than a dozen adults in a living room with our children sitting on the floor in the center. My family has started several of these house churches among English speakers. It is really very simple. But more importantly, we have also encouraged them among Muslim-background disciples and have seen them replicate and spread. When this is our understanding of church, any one of us, and any one of the disciples that we make, can start a church. That is how church-planting movements work. We yearn for every disciple in our church to start their own churches. This dream can become reality when the disciples are using the simple, biblical definition of church.

Now, don't forget where we are going. We are about to look at health strategies. Keep in mind those exciting verses that were quoted in Chapter Four about large numbers of disciples being won and of the Gospel being disseminated across entire regions. As was said, that vision of multiplying indigenous churches will be the endpoint in each of the health strategy possibilities that we discuss.

In 2004, David Garrison greatly advanced the study of these movements in his book, *Church Planting Movements*. One component of the book discussed the characteristics of these movements. To study this, several witnesses of these church-planting movements were gathered. These apostolic workers were asked to write out all of the factors that they felt contributed to the church movement in their area. If they thought the new sound systems put in the church buildings resulted in disciples and churches, that was listed. (By the way, I'm pretty sure that wasn't on anybody's list.) If they thought that a major prayer emphasis made a difference, they put that down.[9]

After the lists were made, 10 elements were found to have been listed by every apostolic worker at the meeting. These 10 elements were (1) prayer, (2) abundant Gospel sowing, (3) intentional church planting, (4) adherence to scriptural authority, (5) local church leadership, (6) lay church leadership, (7) cell or house church format, (8) churches planting churches, (9) rapid church reproduction, and (10) healthy churches.

These 10 elements fall into three distinct categories:

Ten elements universally found in church-planting movements:

1. Prayer 2. Abundant Gospel sowing 3. Intentional church planting	▶	**Ingredients** (What you add)
4. Scriptural authority 5. Local leadership 6. Lay leadership 7. Cell/house format	▶	**Methods** (How you do it)
8. Churches planting churches 9. Rapid reproduction 10. Healthy churches	▶	**Products** (What will result)

If you took high-school chemistry, you can think of elements one through three as the ingredients that the apostolic teams added to the environment. Elements four through seven are the methods by which the apostolic ministers did the work. Elements eight through 10 are the products that resulted from the work. The apostolic ministers themselves were primarily catalysts, which sped up the process and precipitated results.

An important fact about a catalyst is that it is not an ingredient. That is, it doesn't leave any piece of itself behind within the products. A catalyst is essential to make the reaction take place, but it doesn't take part in the reaction. It is an outsider that brings about the reaction without becoming part of it. In chemistry, the most common catalyst is the Bunsen burner, which turns up the heat to make the reaction move faster. Apostolic ministers are catalysts who turn up the heat to make things happen, but they are outsiders who are doing their jobs until they can move on and catalyze another reaction in another place.

Looking more closely at numbers one through three, these are the things that an apostolic team primarily does to make disciples. Team members pray and encourage others to pray to receive that which they need from God to advance the Gospel and to defeat the spiritual powers of opposition. They disseminate the Gospel to as many people as possible using whatever means they can. Their minds are set on the objective of making disciples and gathering them together as a church.

Numbers four through seven refer to how the apostolic team goes about forming the kind of church that is most likely to replicate. As a person is making disciples and forming them into groups, the authority of Scripture is above that of any person or denomination. The method is to use local leadership for the church, to use unpaid and nonprofessional (lay) leaders, and to meet in houses. Some of these house churches may replicate by sending out their own apostolic ministers or some may divide like cells.

Numbers eight through 10 refer to the results. In other words, if you do numbers one through three, in the method of numbers four through seven, success can be determined by looking for numbers eight through 10. If you don't see them, look back through numbers one through seven to find the problem.

If disciples have been made correctly and the church has been properly trained, churches should have a passion and the proper strategy to replicate. In fact, the churches should be starting other churches aggressively and rapidly, even in the face of persecution. Also, the churches should be exhibiting spiritual gifts, giving to the poor, loving one another, etc.

I have broken down these 10 elements in this way to show how simple it all is. Putting the methods and products aside for a moment, there are *only* three things that an apostolic minister or team adds to the mix. Those things are *prayer, abundant Gospel sowing,* and *intentional church planting.* Let that sink in a minute, because it is a key point.

Don't misunderstand the big picture. If you wanted to make sulfuric acid and you put bottles of sulfur, oxygen, and hydrogen on a table next to each other, you wouldn't get your desired product. The way that the apostolic teams utilized the ingredient of *intentional church planting* was the key to their success, thus my great emphasis on the concept of "church" earlier in this chapter. But it is still refreshing to see that there weren't 50, 20, or even 10 ingredients found in these movements of multiplying disciples and churches. There were only three.

Also notice that only the last of these ingredients, *intentional church planting*, absolutely requires presence in the target area. It is possible to induce disciples around the world to pray for a people group without leaving their homes. In the same way, the Gospel can be disseminated, to some degree, through mass media. But intentional church planting cannot be done from a distance. It is *the incarnational element*, it is the primary subject of the book of Acts, and it is the strength of health strategies.

Again, it is important to understand the biblical methodology of church. Elements number four through 10 deal with this crucial issue. We have put it aside for the purposes of this book, but health strategies will never get off the ground if you are effective at incarnational church planting but start a traditional First Something-or-Other Church with red bricks and white columns. You must internalize and practice every aspect of biblical church methodology (I'm talking about house church here) so that you will form churches that are conducive to replication. Please don't study this just as an academic exercise. If you haven't started a house church in your first language, you won't be able to model or give advice on starting one cross-culturally. It is something that every disciple can and should do.

In Chapter Four, I asserted that God revealed the church-planting methodology of Paul for a purpose. I then suggested that Paul's results of the rapid spread of the Gospel across entire regions should also be our objective. But that is not all that can be learned from

Paul's methods. Brief study also demonstrates a simple church-planting template. The three points of this template will become the outline for each of the health strategies in Part Three. To help you understand the importance of these steps, I will liken them to the essentials of farming.

Throughout the world, there are numerous farming techniques. Some farmers plow behind oxen or yaks while others ride atop air-conditioned tractors. Some farmers sow by hand while others use mechanical spreaders. Some farmers depend upon the rain to water their crops while others use irrigation. Despite the various techniques, there are some essentials of farming that are common to all if there is to be a harvest. There must be seeds, these seeds must be sown, and the seeds must have access to water and light.

In the same way, there are some components of church-planting strategy that must be present if a healthy and replicating church is to be realized. These components are essential, because they were revealed to us by God through the church-planting methods of Paul. But they are also essential by logic. Tactics for implementing these points may vary, but the strategic points themselves are always valid and should be followed.

Just a brief look at Paul's methodology allows one to see these simple components. So let's take a look at Paul's work in the city of Iconium:

> The same thing happened in Iconium; *they entered the Jewish synagogue* and spoke in such a way that a great number of both Jews and Greeks believed (Acts 14:1; italics mine).

> So they *stayed there for some time* and spoke boldly (Acts 14:3a; italics mine).

> When an attempt was made by both the Gentiles and Jews, with their rulers, to assault and stone them, they found out about it and fled... (Acts 14:5-6).

... they returned to Lystra, to Iconium, and to Antioch, strengthening the hearts of the disciples by encouraging them ... (Acts 14:21-22; italics mine).

I can tell you now that the key word in the last verse is "disciples." Things didn't always go well for Paul and his team. In fact, in the 15 or so cities where Paul preached, he was in trouble and had resistance to his preaching as often as he had a positive response. So it was good that he could return to a group of disciples.

As has already been established, it is disciples that make up a church. Healthy disciples make up healthy churches, and healthy churches result in church-planting movements. However, getting the *first* disciples, forming these disciples into healthy churches, and encouraging these churches to multiply is much more difficult and dangerous than it sounds on paper.

These disciples did not appear spontaneously. In the beginning, Paul and Barnabas went to this unevangelized city and positioned themselves so as to have an audience for the Gospel. After some people believed, the apostles spent more time with them and modeled bold disciple making. After fleeing the region, they later returned to encourage and strengthen the disciples. This same pattern is repeated many times and was Paul's church-planting strategy. He entered the community, made disciples, and empowered the church.

Steps of Paul's church-planting strategy

1. Enter the community
2. Make disciples
3. Empower the church

These three basic steps are Paul's template for intentional church planting. According to Garrison's findings, intentional church planting, accompanied by prayer and abundant Gospel sowing, was one of the three ingredients cited by those who had witnessed a church movement. Do not forget the importance of prayer and abundant Gospel sowing, but stay with me as we look specifically at intentional church planting and investigate the three steps of church planting that Paul followed.

I realize that these components seem overly simple, but it is common for strategies to get hung up at any of these points. I have met many workers who have been in countries for decades and have never established a church among their people group. Sometimes they seem to be doing everything by the book. But oftentimes they are stuck somewhere on one of these basics. Perhaps they never learned the language and can't communicate the Gospel. Perhaps they didn't make real disciples who have a passion to share their faith. Perhaps they had the same understanding of church that I initially had and were never able to plant a healthy church that multiplies.

As a farmer must know how to sow seeds, each apostolic team must address the components of planting churches, must determine the tactics to implement each component, and must see the job through. It is a difficult task, particularly among those people groups that have not yet been reached with the Gospel. After all, there is some good reason why they are still unreached.

In the example of farming, the most important component, which was not mentioned, is the power of photosynthesis—a component from God, which man cannot provide. Without photosynthesis, a seed would remain a seed, and a seedling would remain a seedling. There would be no growth and no multiplication.

In the same way, let's not forget that the vital component in church planting and church-planting movements is the Spirit of God. We may be able to enter a community on our own, but no one can make disciples on their own. No one can establish the church of God upon the earth without the power of the Holy Spirit. What a wonderful partnership it is when, as in the example of farming, we couple the toil of man with the work of God to produce a harvest.

CHAPTER 6

ENTER THE COMMUNITY

They continued their journey from Perga and reached
Antioch in Pisidia. On the Sabbath day they went into the
synagogue and sat down. After the reading of the Law and
the Prophets, the leaders of the synagogue sent [word] to
them, saying, "Brothers, if you have any message of encouragement for the people, you can speak" (Acts 13:14-15).

*The two doctors arose early and each packed a small backpack with
simple medical supplies. They prayed: "Lord, give us each an opportunity to tell the Gospel today."*

*Their destination was a new disciple's village known for its poverty
and illness. This disciple had shared the Gospel with some family members
there and reported some interest in Jesus and some opposition. Two new
disciples traveled with the doctors as volunteer helpers.*

*The doctors were greeted warmly, but with skepticism. Their arrival
had been expected.*

*They met with the village leaders and explained that they were
working in conjunction with the Ministry of Health to teach preventive
health measures at the village level to reduce illness in the country. This
teaching was best done from house to house with the whole family present. They added that it was difficult to be taught if there was already*

illness in the home and said that they were prepared to see any sick people and write prescriptions for needed medications.

The village leaders were pleased with this idea, especially since every home would receive a free visit from a Western doctor, and they gave their consent to the plan. The doctors had chosen a village with less than 50 homes, estimating that they could visit every home in less than one week. That allowed for considerable time in each home and plenty of time to share the Gospel when the opportunity presented itself.

But the opportunity did not present itself for one doctor, at least not on the first visit. After seeing the sick and teaching how to prevent disease, he forced the conversation toward religion and gave a rather plastic presentation of the Gospel. The family did not interrupt, but was obviously unengaged.

The second home, for this physician, was much the same. He was compassionate and loving when it came to health, but he had an agenda to teach the Gospel. This time he was stopped by the father who stated that they were Muslims.

In the third home, he didn't even try. He was somewhat discouraged that his prayer had not been answered.

The fourth home, however, was completely different. It did not seem to be a home at all. There was just one man, and he was quite lonely.

The man sat in the unlit house and told his physical troubles to the doctor. There didn't seem to be a need for the usual health training, as the teaching was ordinarily directed toward the children or the women who prepared the food. So the doctor was at a loss as to what should be done next.

The helper though, who was a strong disciple in the Lord, asked the man, "Do you have faith in God?"

There was silence as the man pondered this surprising question. "I am a Muslim," he answered. "I do have faith in God."

"Abraham took his son up on to a mountain and offered him as a sacrifice in obedience to the word of the Lord," his countryman replied. "This is true faith. Do you have faith like that?"

The man could not answer.

From that introduction, with the doctor sitting in silence and offering supportive prayer, the disciple explained how Jesus was the real sacrifice and how we must place faith in Him, rather than in works. And another soul was added to the kingdom that day.

CUL-DE-SAC STRATEGIES

An apostolic family is called to an unreached people group and goes to missionary school. Tactics are learned to produce healthy, rapidly reproducing churches. The target people group is in a restricted country, so creative ways to get visas for their team are found. Perhaps the family tells the government that they will open a small business or will have a travel agency. Once they move, they learn the language, mobilize prayer partners, and look for opportunities to share the Gospel through the techniques that they have learned. They also struggle to survive.

Things don't go well. The neighbors aren't really interested in the Gospel. The other Christians in the country, or prayer partners in the sending country, have their own agendas and don't care to join in their work. The whole situation is discouraging.

It's as if their team has climbed over a great wall to get into the country only to face another huge wall ahead and no easy way to cover the distance between the barriers. They are trapped. They do not want to retreat, they cannot breach the barriers before them, and they are completely vulnerable where they are. The spiritual forces of evil are easily firing arrows down on them. The problem is that *creative access* into a country is a dead end if it does not provide a way for the incarnational team to engage in daily disciple making.

Remember that there are three primary steps to intentional church planting: *enter the community*, *make disciples*, and *empower the church*. Although these steps seem simple, each of them must be understood thoroughly. As in the illustration, it helps if you think of these steps as barriers that must be overcome by your team. In addition to the barriers, there is considerable distance between the barriers, sometimes treacherous, which must be traveled by the team before encountering the next barrier.

The step of *enter the community* includes the barrier of getting the appropriate permissions to get into the country and to work among the desired people group. But that is only the beginning. The step is not complete until you open your mouth to make disciples. Here's a peek into the next chapter. In order to make disciples, you must have the capacity to communicate, and your audience must have great respect for you. So, *enter the community* is finished when the first words proceed from your mouth and your audience wants to hear what you have to say. Because this first step is difficult, I have broken it down into three smaller steps called the *ABCs of health strategies*.

THE ABCS

A twelve-year-old female presents to your emergency room by ambulance after a motor-vehicle accident. On gross examination she is immobile and unresponsive, has multiple facial lacerations, and has an obvious puncture wound in the left upper quadrant of her abdomen. Also obvious is a compound fracture of her left lower extremity.

Since you are a general surgeon, you are most concerned with the puncture wound to the abdomen. It is right over the spleen and you have seen similar cases in which the patient has bled to death, internally, within minutes.

Without losing any time you take the patient to surgery. But in the elevator, the heart monitor from the ambulance indicates that the patient has had cardiac arrest. She has died. You search for a cause but can't find anything. After you think about it, you realize that you never saw her breathe. Was she breathing when she came in, and if so, did she stop at some point while you were focused on her abdominal wound?

Don't worry. The scenario above could never happen in a modern emergency room (I hope!). It seems somewhat realistic, however, that a health worker could overlook hidden things, even the absence of breathing, with so many other obvious problems. And it would be possible, if we were not so thoroughly trained, to ignore the blood and obvious injuries and begin every trauma case with the *ABCs of trauma:*

A. First, check the patient's **airway** to make sure that there is no obstruction to breathing.

B. Next make sure the patient is **breathing**, and restart his breathing if he is not.

C. Then move on to the patient's **circulation**, making sure that the heart is beating and that there is no bleeding.

D. Once these things are taken care of, un**dress** the patient to give a thorough examination, and give **drugs** that are needed.

E. Next order **extras**, such as x-ray or laboratory tests.

Commonly, people miss the big picture because of some distraction. Our distractions are occasionally trivial but are often important. An abdominal puncture wound is very serious, but the larger issue is the patient's life. If we stopped the abdominal bleeding but didn't restart breathing, we would have seriously failed our patient. We must stand back and look at all of the issues in order to prioritize appropriately or we must follow a formula, like the *ABCs of Trauma*, that helps us to prioritize.

Now take a look at planet earth. Because of sin, it suffers greatly. Among the multiple consequences of its trauma are hunger and famine; diseases like HIV, tuberculosis, cancer, and leprosy; poverty; and ubiquitous lostness. What is our strategy for helping this new patient? Keep in mind that we lost the last one. Since we were pretending to be a surgeon, we went straight to the bleeding abdomen. If we had been an orthopedic surgeon, we may have gone straight to the compound fracture. A plastic surgeon may have gone straight to the facial lacerations.

Similarly, one's tendency is to filter the ills of the world according to one's own preference or training. A social worker, having seen the crippling consequences of poverty in the undeveloped world, may feel compelled to work within that realm. Likewise, an AIDS nurse may feel compelled to work among AIDS patients. As in the medical example, however, this approach is not asking the question, "What is best for the patient?" Instead it is asking the question, "Where do *I* prefer to start?"

If you have an established ministry focus, you will not likely want to change. *What we want* is not the relevant issue. God is doing what is best for the earth. As His disciples, it is our job to adopt His perspective and to adapt our behavior accordingly. As in the example of the emergency room visit, I hope that you would want to know if your efforts were misdirected and would humbly shift your behavior to focus on what is best for your patient. If a nurse had pointed out that the patient was not breathing, I hope that you would abandon whatever other injury had captured your attention and address the more important issue.

Well, what about this second patient? How do we prioritize so that we can do the absolute best for planet earth and glorify the One for whom we work? So many issues are screaming for attention.

This brings us around to *the ABCs of health strategies*. Remember, the purpose of this formula is to help us fight our natural tendency to only choose an issue that attracts us and to force us to begin in a way that is best for our patient—in this case, an ailing world. So here we go:

A IS FOR *ACCESS THE UNREACHED*

When Paul and Barnabas went out, they were *led by the Spirit*, first to Cyprus and then into Turkey. These destinations were both west of their starting place in Antioch in a direction where the Gospel had never been before. The Spirit did not send them south where the church was already established.

Acts 13:2-4 tells us that this first step in apostolic activity was through the leading of the Holy Spirit, but the premise that the Gospel must always be advanced into unreached places became a cornerstone of Paul's methodology. In fact, he stated quite plainly that this was always his practice. In Romans he wrote: "So my aim is to evangelize where Christ has not been named, in order that I will not be building on someone else's foundation, but, as it is written: Those who had no report of Him will see, and those who have not heard will understand" (Romans 15:20-21).

Not all of Paul's behavior was inspired by the Holy Spirit. Just like anyone, he made plenty of mistakes. But I maintain that this practice of advancing the Gospel forward was not from Paul's flesh, but was intentionally inspired by the Holy Spirit to be incorporated into apostolic methodology today.

Remember my argument from Chapter Four. Out of all of the apostolic activity of the day, God chose to share with us what Paul did and how. He then inspired Paul to define this part of his methodology in the above verses. In fact, in Romans 15:23-24a , Paul said, "But now I no longer have any work to do in these provinces, and I have strongly desired for many years to come to you whenever I travel to Spain."

Obviously, Paul's team had not presented the Gospel to every person in every town that they had visited. We know that they had not planted churches or even visited all of the towns of that region. Yet, Paul considered his job done in those provinces. His team had established healthy churches, and they trusted these new disciples to complete the task in those provinces.

The remaining unreached regions of the world are hard to get to and unfriendly to outsiders or outside ideas. It is obviously the desire and work of God for all peoples to know of His glory. Here are a few of my favorite verses on that subject:

> All the nations You have made will come and bow down before You, Lord, and will honor Your name (Psalms 86:9; italics mine).

> … all the distant coastlands of the nations will bow in worship to Him, each in its own place (Zephaniah 2:11b; italics mine).

> For the earth will be filled with the knowledge of the LORD's glory, as the waters cover the sea (Habakkuk 2:14; italics mine).

"I will shake *all the nations* so that the treasures of *all the nations* will come, and I will fill this house with glory," says the LORD of Hosts (Haggai 2:7; italics mine).

"For My name will be great *among the nations*, from the rising of the sun to its setting. Incense and pure offerings will be presented in My name *in every place* because My name will be great *among the nations*," says the LORD of Hosts (Malachi 1:11; italics mine).

This good news of the kingdom will be proclaimed in all the world as a testimony to all nations. And then the end will come (Matthew 24:14; italics mine).

Go, therefore, and make disciples of *all nations*, baptizing them in the name of the Father and of the Son and of the Holy Spirit (Matthew 28:19; italics mine).

... *all the nations* will come and worship before You, because Your righteous acts have been revealed (Revelation 15:4; italics mine).

All of the nations will worship God, but they cannot know Him without knowing Jesus and the Gospel. Therefore, the highest priority is to advance the Gospel to regions and ethnic groups with no access to the Gospel so that all nations will know about the greatness of God and salvation.

Yes, many nations will be abandoned by apostolic ministers once the church is established in an area. This biblical practice is necessary to advance the Gospel to the ends of the earth. *Entering the community* begins here. We can trust the Lord to continue to work through those churches that He has established.

WHERE TO START

The book of Acts is non-stop action, relating tales of average people who do extraordinary things for Christ through faith and His power. I must admit, however, for the longest time I thought it unfair that the apostles had some mystical connection to the Spirit of God that we do not have. After all, the book indicates that they primarily received their directions from the Holy Spirit.

I gained insight after I became an apostolic worker in an area that was totally out of my comfort zone. Since I had no idea how to function in that new world, I began to rely much more on the Holy Spirit, and dramatic things began to happen. As one begins to operate through faith, something of a *spiritual zone* is entered. Your brain isn't turned off, and you usually don't hear voices telling you which way to go. In my experience, we persevered forward in prayer and found ourselves moving beyond great obstacles and towards an end that would bring more glory to God.

After these events, when I would relate one of our stories to a church or to a friend, I would often find myself saying the same words as the book of Acts: "Then the Spirit led us to…" On more than one occasion, I was asked if I had heard the literal voice of God or to explain what was meant by this statement. The point is that the experience can't be explained well. At the time, the options before us were dark and ominous. In retrospect, after we had moved forward in faith, we could see clearly the guidance of the Lord.

Choosing the right community to enter, therefore, requires spiritual guidance, but this can be difficult to discern. My family once worked among a people group resistant to the Gospel. Years later, though, there was a massive earthquake which came during a Muslim holiday. This troubled the people. Why had God sent destruction upon them during a time that should have been holy? Because of this act of God, they were not able to fulfill the obligations of that holiday and properly worship God. It was as if God did not want them to follow through with religious practice. As a result, people became more open to hearing about Jesus.

An important consideration in choosing the right unevangelized community is a major change such as an earthquake, war, or political struggle. During difficulty, people may question the foundation of their beliefs. Remember that it is God who brings about these events.

Another indication that God is at work is the presence of spontaneous disciples in a community. Frequently, in places where the Gospel has never been preached, you will find disciples in remote places. When you ask how they came to faith, you are in for a real treat. Each story is a little miracle of how the sovereign Lord had singled out that person, and perhaps the spouse or friend, to hear the Gospel.

In addition to disciples, it is not uncommon to find a "man of peace" in a community, another great indication that God is at work. The concept of the man of peace comes from Luke 10:5: "Whatever house you enter, first say, 'Peace to this household.' If a son of peace is there, your peace will rest on him; but if not, it will return to you. Remain in the same house, eating and drinking what they offer" (Luke 10:5-7a).

There is only one verse in the Bible about this person of peace, but meeting an individual that fits this label is common among apostolic ministers. In my experience, a man of peace usually finds you and your team, and he greatly appreciates what you are doing in his community. In fact, his appreciation is almost irrational. He will miss work, spend much of his time, make capital donations, and give all manner of verbal praise to you and your team. And he will never tire of doing so.

In one place we called our person "man of peace" to his face, and he relished the title. He took us inside many government offices to help us get permission to access the restricted mountains, and each time he would brag that we called him the "man of peace."

At the same time, most of us have found that our men of peace, although they show interest in the Gospel, don't necessarily make the plunge of giving their entire life to Christ. Yet, they open up the doors of the community. Also keep in mind that God may send you a woman of peace who has influence in the community and desires to help you succeed.

Another way to see if God is at work in a community is the presence of signs or wonders. As an example, a friend was learning the local language and wandered into the small hospital of his town for language practice with the patients. He visited with six men who naturally wanted to talk about their physical problems. He asked if he could pray for healing through the name of Christ. When he went back to the hospital three days later, he was waylaid by a group of young men with many questions, since all six men had been healed. Frankly, they were angry—not at my friend, but at their religious leaders. They had been told that Christianity was a false religion, but now they had seen miracles.

Coincidently, I was there on the day that my friend returned to the hospital, so I can attest that this story is valid. I did not see the men before they were healed, but I saw them afterwards and can tell you that there was great commotion over the event.

There are other issues that can also be considered in deciding which community to enter. Keeping in mind that your primary objective is to determine the leading of the Spirit, a practical tool that can help you is offered below, adapted from another Great Commission organization:

Disciples present?	-5	-4	-3	-2	-1	0	1	2	3	4	5
Man of peace?	-5	-4	-3	-2	-1	0	1	2	3	4	5
Signs and wonders?	-5	-4	-3	-2	-1	0	1	2	3	4	5
Spiritually open?	-5	-4	-3	-2	-1	0	1	2	3	4	5
Volunteerism possible?	-5	-4	-3	-2	-1	0	1	2	3	4	5
Live close to the community?	-5	-4	-3	-2	-1	0	1	2	3	4	5
Community desires program?			-3	-2	-1	0	1	2	3		
Many needy people?			-3	-2	-1	0	1	2	3		
Invitation to come there?			-3	-2	-1	0	1	2	3		

You can use this tool as it is, or make your own tool. You may feel that some issues are very important, while some are not important at all, so you can weigh the issues accordingly. If you think that the presence of signs and wonders is very, very important, then you can rank it as high as a positive 10 if it is present and as low as a negative 10 if it is absent. Likewise, if you do not believe in miracles in this day, then you can remove it from your list altogether. A problem, however, may occur when you find a community in which the miracle that you have been seeking has occurred, but it is a six-hour drive from your house.

In general, it is a good idea to pick out many potential communities and spend dozens of hours investigating and praying in each. Take lots of notes and after your evaluation time is over, use the tool to help you choose the community in which you will begin your work. If you look at the criteria in the tool, they are mostly spiritual issues. Because you prayed and looked for God at work, you can still say that you were led by the Spirit in your decisions, even though you used a tool to help you organize what you have learned.

B IS FOR *BEHIND CLOSED DOORS*

Jesus entered communities on foot and did not need a visa. He did not ask permission of local authorities to begin any work. He began his work by healing, which gave him credibility and gathered crowds for his teaching. In many cases, Jesus stayed out from town, perhaps to avoid the entanglements of gathering assemblies without a permit. But think about Jesus' platform for preaching. It was first built upon His identity as a healer and was then supported through the quality of His teaching.

This is a huge lesson for us. Your platform for ministry is not based upon what you call yourself but upon how the community sees you. We have a tendency to get this backwards. The business cards that we pass out and the things that we call ourselves are not what make up the foundation of our disciple making. That platform is based upon our identity as it is perceived by the community. I have known medical apostles who had labored for years among downtrodden communities who were referred to as "holy people" because of their dedication to the needy and their insight into physical illnesses.

Consequently, they could go anywhere they wanted, and everyone listened when they spoke. Identity as a "holy person" was the platform for making disciples, not their label as a missionary or the title on their business cards.

One's platform for ministry is based upon his identity as it is perceived by the community.

When a person has a dual identity, he is either seen by the community as being mentally ill or involved in some kind of deception. In the same way, an incarnational worker who gets a visa through one identity but uses another identity to try to *make disciples* will illicit immediate skepticism from the host community. In addition, the worker will also be in a constant tension of forcing disciple-making opportunities while trying to protect his visa.

Unfortunately, this is done all of the time by well-meaning workers. Because a visa doesn't sanction a position to make disciples, but disciple making is pursued, the worker lives in a world of dissonance. Trying to live a double life, the worker eventually tells small lies to neighbors and local authorities. When asked why you are in a country, you should be able to give the same answer to every person with honesty. You should be qualified for the job that you say you do and should be working at that job week after week.

Years ago we had arrived in a completely Muslim country where we were soon approached by two young men. They identified themselves as converts to Christianity and asked if we could teach them more about Jesus. There had been one other apostolic worker in the region for over a year named Robert, so I asked them why they had never gone to Robert for teaching.

"We don't like Robert," they replied. "He tells everyone he is a businessman, but he never does any business. He just rides around passing out tracts and talking about Jesus."

I was amazed. For a year they had wanted to learn more about Jesus and were in the same town with a guy that they said was a renowned evangelist, but they wouldn't approach him. To them, he was off limits because he lacked integrity. Over the coming months, we were told by many disciples that they didn't like or didn't trust Robert. A platform of trust will be the foundation upon which you begin making disciples behind closed doors.

INTIMATE CONVERSATION

Evangelistic crusades and traditional churches are constructed in such a way as to provide the best possible context for communication. The organizers try to think of every detail and then design a program in which the audience most likely will be impacted by the information heard. Friendly greeters, comfortable seating, lighting, clear acoustics, singing, and testimonials pave the way for a positive experience. Finally, the chief communicator will be appropriately dressed and inviting in his opening words.

Perhaps there is a point when this preparation becomes disproportionately emphasized, but that does not mean that the premise that the Gospel should be presented in a comfortable environment is invalid. Let me stop playing around with Western models and show you how important this is for apostolic ministers.

If your target people are Muslim, Buddhist, Hindu, Communist, etc., they are not culturally allowed to listen to a presentation about an alternate religion. No matter how interested they may be in the content of your message, they cannot easily listen to your words unless the context makes them feel secure. Just as Nicodemus came to Jesus at night, even the most ardent seekers after truth want to be cloaked during their investigative stage. They know that listening to the Gospel is taboo and will take protective measures.

In many cultures, religion is determined by birth and is to be maintained by everyone in the community. It is believed that strength and well-being come from a unity of belief about God, and outside teachings and ideas are not only unwelcome, but they are considered dangerous to the community, like a small cancer that threatens the larger host.

Just as skin protects the human body from cancer, there are barriers around the outside of the community to prevent these cancer-like teachings from entering. Most of these outside barriers come in the form of laws and social rules. Outsiders are not allowed easily into the country, have more difficulty entering into a community, and even more difficulty getting repeated visits to homes.

As the human body has immune cells that kill cancer cells, there are internal protectors inside countries and communities. The police, community, and religious leaders watch to make sure that no outsider penetrates the barriers in order to disseminate teaching that is harmful to the body. They are always on the trail of missionaries and preachers and will eventually find those who are successful in the *cancerous* plan to multiply.

If a cancer does penetrate the outside barriers, avoids the internal defenses, attaches itself, and begins to multiply within the body, then it is much easier to find. The strategy of the body, at this point, is to destroy the cancer and eliminate it from the body. In the same way, if you preach often, they may not find you, but if disciples are made and baptized, they will find out about it and will keep investigating until they find the source. Furthermore, they will do whatever is socially appropriate to destroy the new disciples by intimidation, open criticism, threats, arrests, and possible torture or murder. These latter interventions are not as common, but the threat and fear of such is very effective in preventing the multiplication of disciples. It is hoped that this attack will separate the disciples and prevent a cancerous church from being established.

Every inhabitant in a community is aware of the essentials of the above paradigm. When you begin to speak about a new teaching that is not consistent with the religion or laws of their community, they know you to be potentially dangerous to the community. Their decision to risk listening and learning from you has much to do with two things. First, they are not likely to listen to you without the prodding of the Holy Spirit. But even if the Holy Spirit is drawing them, they will take a look at the environment before deciding if they will listen. If they determine the context to be secure, and they want to learn from you, effective communication has a good chance. But if you are speaking in a place where they think that others can overhear your conversation, effective communication is much less likely to occur. You can talk, but they will always be looking over a shoulder to make sure that they are not found out.

You must learn about your people and discover the best context in which to share the Gospel. In some places it is best to share with one family at a time at the home. In other places, you may be able to share with two or three people at a time in a park or other public location.

Getting behind real closed doors isn't necessary among every people group and isn't what is really meant by "B is for behind closed doors." Sometimes it is even possible to present the Gospel to groups. The point is that the intimate conversation needed for disciple making only takes place in an environment that is considered safe by your audience. Remember that the practice of teaching in homes was common for Jesus and was also carried on by the apostles as shown in these verses:

> Every day in the temple complex, and *in various homes*, they continued teaching and proclaiming the good news that the Messiah is Jesus (Acts 5:42; italics mine).

> … I did not shrink back from proclaiming to you anything that was profitable, or from teaching it to you in public and from *house to house* (Acts 20:20; italics mine).

A good strategy, therefore, will get you and your disciple makers into many of these intimate settings every day. It will also give you opportunity to go back inside homes on more than one occasion. Once inside, you may have the opportunity to witness to five or more family members. If your team were to share in just one such home each day, it is possible that 100 people could hear the Gospel in one month, assuming a five-day work week. This may not be possible in every situation, so these numbers are just to help reinforce the principle. Good strategies get disciple makers behind closed doors every day. Strategies that don't provide this simply do not measure up.

C IS *CARE FOR THE NEEDY*

This step is still a part of *enter the community* and directly precedes
the making of disciples. It is important because it will give integrity
as you start to communicate the Gospel, but that is not the only
reason to do this. Remember, we do not meet physical needs *so that*
we can make disciples. We do both ministries together, because that
is what Jesus commanded and modeled. We must care for the needy
in homes with no strings attached. After helping, if the family has
no interest in hearing about Jesus, move on. You have done the right
thing by caring for the needy. As you continue in this manner, it is
very likely that the Lord will provide you with opportunities to share
His message. Here are some verses that demonstrate this:

> As Peter was traveling from place to place, he also came
> down to the saints who lived in Lydda. There he found
> a man named Aeneas, who was paralyzed and had been
> bedridden for eight years. Peter said to him, "Aeneas,
> Jesus Christ heals you. Get up and make your own bed,"
> and immediately he got up. So all who lived in Lydda and
> Sharon saw him and turned to the Lord (Acts 9:32-35).

> Then Peter sent them all out of the room. He knelt down,
> prayed, and turning toward the body said, "Tabitha, get
> up!" She opened her eyes, saw Peter, and sat up. He gave
> her his hand and helped her stand up. Then he called the
> saints and widows and presented her alive. This became
> known throughout all Joppa, and many believed in the
> Lord (Acts 9:40-42).

Over the years, we have known many who have been brought
in by the local authorities for questioning. Those on business plat-
forms are asked the same question: "Where are your books?" After
all, a businessman always keeps good records and should be making
a sizeable profit. Otherwise it wouldn't make sense for him to be in

the country. Other friends, perhaps on tourist visas, have also had no good answers when questioned about their presence in the country or their activity. When you enter restricted countries, you give those governments a reason for your visit, so do those things that you promised.

Most likely, you *will* be scrutinized if you are successful in making disciples. You should look forward to the day that you are brought in for questioning. Work in such a way that you can afford to be successful. You will more likely survive the scrutiny.

In one place, we worked among the poor and made a few disciples. Soon thereafter, though, a report came out in the newspaper that 50 families had converted to Christianity in that small town. I wish. Apparently, someone complained and the authorities began to investigate the matter. They reasoned that the Gospel could only have entered the area through foreigners, so they paid each of us a visit. One family, doing business in the area, was asked if they had passed out Bibles or proselytized. After the investigation, they were given one week to leave the country. A nearby family, working with another people group, left the country to avoid the questions. Our medical team was raked over the coals. They interviewed us for hours, but they never asked about Bibles or apostolic activity. We showed them our records of treating thousands of poor villagers and giving free medicines, and this seemed to pacify them. The next day I went to the official and told him that we would leave the country if they wanted. "No, no, Doctor," he replied. "We love you here. But someone has complained, and we had to check up on things."

For years I thought it was a miracle. In hours of interviews, they had never asked us if we had given out Bibles or spoken about Christ. We certainly would not have lied about either of those things, but they never asked. I was relating the story to a disciple from that country, though, and he said, "This was no miracle. Everyone in the area knew what you were doing, but they loved your medical work. So they never asked the questions that could get you in trouble, and they told the complainers that the matter had been investigated thoroughly, and you were not at fault."

Let me catch you up on where we are: *Enter the community* is the first step of intentional church planting and is also the first of three barriers that must be crossed as an apostolic ministry team works toward a disciple-making movement. It begins from the moment one steps foot into the country and ends the moment one opens his mouth to *make disciples*. Getting in the country is not *entering the community*. Simply getting into the country would be like climbing a great wall with no plan on how to cover the treacherous distance to the next barrier. *Entering the community* includes the wall and all of the ground between it and the next wall. *Entering the community* will:

- Allow sustained access to the target areas of the country.
- Allow the apostolic team and national workers repeated access to an intimate environment—usually inside nationals' houses.
- Allow for training of national workers.
- Provide a platform of integrity within the target communities.

The vignette at the beginning of this chapter is a great example of properly *entering the community* and clearly followed *the ABCs*. The doctors were in the country, in the community, and going from house to house telling everyone the same story: "We are charity workers helping people in the remote villages." This story is the same as their agreement with the government, and they worked at it daily.

Because integrity was intact, people eagerly invited them into their houses to hear what they had to say, even about spiritual matters. After all, in their estimation, anyone who has control over physical illnesses must also have insight into spiritual matters. Most important is that the work was a partnership with unpaid national disciple makers. They were capitalizing on the skills of the doctors so that they could enter unreached communities and make disciples.

But what if you are not a doctor or nurse? Can you still enter the community effectively and reach the aforementioned objectives? After you drop over the first barrier into your target country, can you cover the ground of *entering the community* so that you are positioned to make disciples?

Of course you can. None of the original apostles had any formal training. The key is in listening to your people and meeting needs that they perceive as important. The last part of this book will show many ways that this can be done. The D and E of health strategies, *make disciples* and *empower the church*, will be addressed in the next two chapters.

The ABCs of Health Strategies	Church Planting Steps
A is "access unreached areas" B is "behind closed doors" C is "care for the needy"	**Enter the Community**
D is "make disciples"	**Make Disciples**
E is "empower the church"	**Empower the Church**

CHAPTER 7

MAKE DISCIPLES

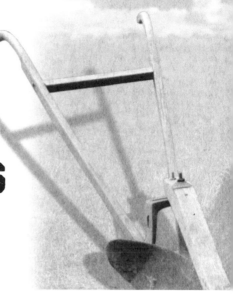

"… they had evangelized that town and made many disciples" (Acts 14:21).

It was fascinating to sit with 12 disciples from Muslim backgrounds and listen to each answer the question, "How did you come to faith in Jesus Christ?" I had known and watched their progress as disciples for a year, and yet their stories were not consistent with my observations. Much more had gone on inside of them than I had ever seen on the outside.

"I first discovered Jesus in the Bible," one of the men responded. "I was brokenhearted over the war and great difficulties here, and had tried being a better Muslim. Despite many prayers and sacrifices, I did not experience any relief from inner turmoil. Then one day, I was secretly given a Bible by a friend. I did not think much of the gift, but I decided to read it in my room. I didn't know where to start. I thumbed through several passages and read this remarkable statement by Jesus: 'Come to Me, all of you who are weary and burdened, and I will give you rest. All of you, take up My yoke and learn from Me, because I am gentle and humble in heart, and you will find rest for yourselves. For My yoke is easy and My burden is light' (Matthew 11:28-30).

"Immediately I knew that this statement was true, and I believed in Jesus. At that point, however, I was not really a Christian.

"I began to study about Jesus and volunteered to help a medical team in the mountains. I put off baptism because I was scared. Eventually I was baptized, and everyone in my family found out about it. People in the community pressured my parents to send me out of the house. I was not allowed to visit. But I still was not a real Christian, because sometimes people would ask me in the street if I was a Muslim, and I would say 'yes' out of fear. But to Christians, I said that I was a Christian.

"After that, things got very difficult. I was telling my friends about Jesus and we met several times each week to study the Bible and talk about ways to tell Muslims about Jesus. We began to receive many threats. I received death threats by phone in the middle of the night and threatening letters from religious leaders. People even accused us openly.

"I decided that the opposition was too much to bear. I prayed to God and told Him that I would always cherish Jesus in my heart, but I would have to keep it to myself. From that day forward, I determined to live life just like everyone else in my Muslim community on the outside, but be a Christian on the inside.

"I tried to live like that, but it was wrong. Everything inside of me told me that I could not deny Jesus. I had to make a decision.

"I decided that even if everything was taken from me or I was tortured or killed, I would never deny Jesus again. I decided to talk about Jesus to anyone who would listen. That was the day that I overcame my fear of death. That's when I became a real Christian."

"Disciple" may be the biggest little word in any language. There are some short definitions, but the impact of the word cannot really be understood without studying the entire New Testament.

Many churches have a "discipleship program" in which members learn information about the Bible and Christianity and hope to grow in some way. The unspoken expectation is that they will achieve the spiritual level of a disciple. But compare this practice with Acts 14:21: "... they ... evangelized that town and made many disciples."

According to many verses in Acts, the people who came to faith were considered disciples without going through a training course. They were disciples from the moment that they gave up all rights to their future and submitted themselves to the authority of Christ as their Lord. In fact, the term "discipleship" is not found anywhere in the Bible.

Perhaps the problem is with the way the Gospel is usually presented. We commonly ask hearers to "accept Christ," another phrase that you will not find in the New Testament. If you harvest Christians who prayed some prayer to "accept" Christ, but need to take them through a training process to make them into real disciples, you will never get to a movement of the Gospel. Church-planting movements run on healthy churches made up of authentic disciples. In unhealthy churches, you would spend all of your time trying to get half of the people saved. There would be no time for multiplication. The lost half would be holding back the saved half.

Almost 85 percent of Americans label themselves as "Christian." On any given Sunday, however, less than 20 percent of Americans worship God with a church. If you make these kinds of Christians, you will either end up with less than one-fourth of these people meeting with a church or each of these Christians meeting with the church less than one out of every four weeks. That means that if you made 12 Christians, you would have a church of three people. But if you made 12 disciples, as Jesus did, you will have set in place the mechanics to spread the Gospel throughout your entire target region. No amount of persecution or malevolent spiritual force can dissuade the church of authentic disciples from multiplying.

Good strategy development requires that you know where you are and where you are going. Think again about the image of the three barriers with the intervening ground, and remember that the last barrier is *empowering the church*. If you do not *enter the community* properly, you will not be positioned to *make disciples*. In the same way, at this point in strategy development, if you do not make *authentic* disciples, you will not be positioned to *empower the church*. Your church will consist of the poorly committed, and you will be frustrated as an American pastor when you try to empower them to reach their region for Christ.

An authentic disciple, on the other hand, does not need to be prodded to replicate. His passion is the same as that of the Holy Spirit, and he is constantly developing the mind of Christ. He finds practical ways to reach out to family, friends, community, and nation. Some disciples will even come forward and speak of a calling to reach neighboring people groups. Without any special training courses, an authentic disciple has the heart of a disciple maker.

The word disciple is used nearly 300 times in the New Testament and, interestingly, only about 28 of those times refer to a single disciple. Even instances of the single "disciple" are usually pointing out that a disciple, who was still in a group, did or said something in particular. In fact, there are only a few biblical examples of disciples being out alone. As disciples, we are not lone rangers. We need each other for encouragement and synergy.

The apostles taught the disciples to gather together into groups, called churches, and taught them how to worship and minister. The New Testament teaches us the same thing. This inspired teaching from our Lord is incorporated into the behavior of a disciple. Evangelism, the teachings of the apostles, leadership development, apostolic ministry, and even church formation are all found within the simple word *disciple*. I told you it was special.

This is why I use the terms disciple movement, disciple-making movement, and church-planting movement interchangeably. Every disciple is a disciple maker, every disciple gathers with others into a church, and every church of disciples multiplies. When you get real disciples, you get it all.

Authentic disciples are the building blocks of church-planting movements.

To get these disciples, though, an apostolic team's strategy must provide a venue for disciple making. For a disciple to give his future to Christ, he must hear the Gospel. For a disciple to learn how to replicate, he must see others making disciples. For a disciple to learn how to survive scrutiny and persecution, he must see the apostolic team doing the same thing and incorporate the teachings of Jesus into his life. Disciples must be able to see their mentors working among the people, sharing the Gospel of salvation, and relying upon God for all ministry needs. They must also receive personal teaching and correction, and in this way, they are encouraged to become effective ministers of the Gospel themselves. A good strategy must provide an opportunity for all of these aspects of disciple making. It can't just give an apostolic team one day in a community and then move on.

REAL ENGAGEMENT

In the picture above, the little gear is assigned to turn the big gear. It has even gotten close to the big gear. Right now, however, it is irrelevant to the big gear except, perhaps, as a neighboring curiosity. It can spin, make a noise, or change colors, but it is not relevant and is not engaged until it touches and tries to move the larger gear.

In the same way, an apostolic team that moves into a community but isn't able to engage in disciple making is irrelevant to that community from an eternal standpoint. The team members are simply raising their families in a foreign country, a scenario which neither they nor their sending agencies ever envisioned.

The key concept in *making disciples* is that of *communication*. This word does not mean the same thing as just talking or broadcasting information. You can talk to your cat all that you want, but it is not likely that you are communicating except when you call her to dinner.

In this context, the word "communicate" means that information has been transferred to such a degree that it has the potential to result in changed behavior. Of course, you may communicate effectively and your audience may reject the information that you have transferred. But if information passed clearly, and there was the *potential* for your audience to be changed by what they had received, real communication took place. Disciple making begins with authentic communication. Paul stated it plainly in Romans 10:14: "But how can they call on Him in whom they have not believed? And how can they believe without hearing about Him?"

The quality of the transfer of information is not the only important factor in communication or in disciple making. There may be many factors involved. For example, as was intimated in the last chapter, the integrity of the communicator is a vital component. If the audience doesn't like the messenger, they are less likely to hear what he says.

Prejudices on the part of the audience must also be taken into consideration. The most common response that I get to the Gospel is, "You are a Westerner, and this is what you believe, but we have our own religion here." In fact, I have seen a few instances where audiences were surprised when they saw apostolic teams of Koreans or Brazilians because they had thought that Christianity was an American religion.

Effective disciple making is primarily dependent upon effective communication.

When an audience hears the Gospel coming from someone closer to their own culture, communication is more likely to occur. In my opinion, the last resort for a disciple-making team in Asia or Africa is what I call "TWG" or "two white guys." TWGs have their place and are often our only option, but the transfer of the Gospel is most likely to result in changed behavior when the audience can better relate to the speaker. There are exceptions, especially when gifted evangelists are involved, but this is a general rule.

There is another factor that has nothing to do with the context, the communicator, or the quality of the communication. Every evangelist and apostolic worker can tell you stories of mutilating their presentation of the Gospel, but the audience was eager to repent and become disciples. On the contrary, they also have even more stories of speaking eloquently in an ideal environment but being rewarded with blank stares and apathy. Most people simply do not have the *spiritual ears* required to hear and be changed by the message of grace. Even when effective communication takes place, there is not always a correlation between the quality of that communication and the outcome. So it looks like there is something else at work.

The bottom line of the last chapter was that *entering the community* is a spiritual activity, and that trend continues into this chapter. Evangelism, the sharing of the good message, is also a spiritual activity. You can do everything in the best possible manner and have no response to the Gospel. In fact, as we saw in Jesus' ministry and as He taught, you should come to expect that the majority of people will not respond to your message. You cannot draw anyone into the kingdom. Only the Holy Spirit can do that. But at the same time, no one can enter into the kingdom without the Gospel. "It is God's power for salvation to everyone who believes" (Romans 1:16). Keep in mind that God is working in the lives of His elect among every ethnic group before you show up. He will continue to draw them to Himself and will use you as His disciple and instrument, even if your communication ability is still improving.

CHAPTER 8

EMPOWER THE CHURCH

"He [Paul] traveled through Syria and Cilicia, strengthening the churches" (Acts 15:41).

"Hello, Sir. How are you and your family? I'm sorry I don't have time to come in, but there is an important meeting today. It is for all of the Christian workers here."

That was the extent of the message. I had no idea what to expect at such a meeting. The only other meeting for all Christian workers was one that I had called one year prior. At that time, only six other people had shown up, and only one of them had been a national of that area. The meeting had been in English and wasn't a real success. Now the national disciples were inviting me to their meeting.

I arrived a few minutes late, expecting everyone else to be much later, but I found that a heated discussion was already taking place. The warm and noisy room contained 30 men seated on the carpet in a circle. I was the only expatriate in the room, although about half of the men were not from this people group. I knew most of them, but not all.

"Let us all agree," one of my friends was saying in the national language, "that there will be no such thing as a secret believer. If anyone wants to be a part of us, he must never deny that he is a follower of Jesus."

"Yes," several men said. "We can all agree on that."

"And we must also be bold in our witness," said another. "We cannot hide our light under a bushel."

"We must also find a way to spread the Gospel out to the other provinces," said another.

The level of excitement and boldness in the room was beyond measure. Where was all of this power coming from? Every aspect of the conversation would have been considered treasonous by the Muslim community outside, and yet all of them were in agreement—very loud and animated agreement.

I would not have been surprised if the ground had shaken and tongues of fire had appeared on their heads. Just as a newborn pony struggles to its feet and is soon galloping, I was watching power surge through these young disciples.

Identical twins look the same and have many similar characteristics due to identical DNA. If identical twins were separated at birth, however, and were subjected to two radically different environments, they would have different patterns of behavior as adults. A child who was raised to be productive, in contrast to his twin who was raised to find the easy way in life, would be more likely to be productive. The power of DNA is great, and it can overcome many obstacles, but our experiences and training are also important in shaping our personalities.

Don't forget that we are still talking about the incarnational element of *intentional church planting*. I have said that one must intentionally *enter the community*, must intentionally *make disciples*, and now I assert that an apostolic team must also be intentional about *empowering the church*. The primary empowering source for any aspect of kingdom work is the Holy Spirit. At first glance, this may appear to be a contradiction, but it really isn't.

Two great medical terms apply here. Something that is *endogenous* is generated from inside of a person. For example, we have many endogenous hormones that come from our thyroid, pituitary, adrenal, and other glands. An injection of a hormone generated from outside of your body, though, would be called *exogenous*.

As in the example of the twins, the personality of the church is dependent upon two factors. Just as DNA is an endogenous power source that is working within us, the Holy Spirit is also working within the lives of the disciples, urging them to complete their purpose of glorifying God by making more disciples. At the same time, the church needs training to learn how to defer to that power source and how they should structure themselves. This training does not come from inside of the disciples but is exogenous, being administered through teaching. This is where the latter elements that were found to be universal in church-planting movements are important. Those elements are:

- Scriptural authority
- Local leadership
- Lay leadership
- Cell/house format
- Churches planting churches
- Rapid reproduction
- Healthy churches

When an incarnational team *empowers the church*, they fashion the church, as a parent fashions a child, to incorporate these elements and other biblical teachings into the life of the church. An example of this is found in Acts 14:21b-23 during Paul and Barnabas' first missionary trip: "They returned to Lystra, to Iconium, and to Antioch, *strengthening* the hearts of the disciples by *encouraging* them to continue in the faith, and by *telling them*, 'It is necessary to pass through many troubles on our way into the kingdom of God.' When they had *appointed* elders in every church and prayed with fasting, they committed them to the Lord in whom they had believed" (HCSB; italics mine).

When the Holy Spirit enters a disciple, He changes his spiritual DNA. I do not mean this literally, as there is no biblical reference to "spiritual DNA," but think of this as a figurative idea. An authentic disciple is transformed so that he loses passion for comfort and the things of this world, and he takes on the passion of God to glorify His name among the nations. This transformation takes place from the inside out because of the working of the Holy Spirit within.

Notice that Paul and Barnabas recognized the power of the Holy Spirit to complete the work that He had begun. They entrusted the church, a group of disciples, to the Lord rather than committing them to their teachings, a priest, a seminary, or any man-made entity. Through this act they were *empowering the church*. The power that would raise the church was not exogenous but from inside of each disciple. It would be the Holy Spirit in each of them, an endogenous power source, which would cause them to meet, grow, and have a passion to multiply.

In addition to trusting the Holy Spirit, the verse shows us that Paul and Barnabas were also active in fashioning the church through strengthening, encouraging, and appointing elders. These forms of empowerment did not come from within the disciples through their spiritual DNA, but were exogenous, coming by way of more mature disciples. This is equivalent to the way in which a child, in addition to being formed by DNA, is also influenced by parents and environment. These means of empowering the church were the usual practice by Paul and his associates, as you can see by the following verses:

... For a whole year they met with the church and taught large numbers ... (Acts 11:26).

Both Judas and Silas, who were also prophets themselves, encouraged the brothers and strengthened them with a long message (Acts 15:32).

He [Paul] set out, traveling through one place after another in the Galatian territory and Phrygia, strengthening all the disciples (Acts 18:23).

On the first day of the week, we assembled to break bread. Paul spoke to them, and since he was about to depart the next day, he extended his message until midnight (Acts 20:7).

Strengthening the church primarily comes in the form of teaching. Here are two more examples of how Paul stayed among the people for a considerable time, empowering them through his teaching:

> Many of the Corinthians, when they heard, believed and were baptized. Then the Lord said to Paul in a night vision, "Don't be afraid, but keep on speaking and don't be silent. For I am with you, and no one will lay a hand on you to hurt you, because I have many people in this city." And he stayed there a year and six months, teaching the word of God among them (Acts 18:8b-11).

> [Paul] met separately with the disciples, conducting discussions every day in the lecture hall of Tyrannus. And this went on for two years, so that all the inhabitants of the province of Asia, both Jews and Greeks, heard the word of the Lord (Acts 19:9b-10).

In addition to teaching, the importance of the empowering act of encouragement cannot be overemphasized. When the apostles heard about the gathering of disciples in Antioch, their first move was to send Barnabas, whose name means "son of encouragement." "When he [Barnabas] arrived and saw the grace of God, he was glad, and he encouraged all of them to remain true to the Lord with a firm resolve of the heart" (Acts 11:23).

Because we listen to Satan's voice and are afraid, many of us shrink back and do not produce for the kingdom. All fear comes from Satan. So think about the beautiful word "encouragement." When others are timid and afraid to move forward, we have an opportunity to transfer *courage* to them, which we have accumulated through maturity. Encouragement is simply giving courage to others.

I do not believe it to be a coincidence that Barnabas also encouraged Saul to join the church at Antioch, and that the church then went on to impact the entire world by sending out apostles. Without Barnabas' encouragement, there is no evidence that we would have ever heard from Saul in Tarsus again.

Also remember how Barnabas rallied around John Mark, even after he had failed the team of apostles once, and encouraged him to return to apostolic activity. Would Mark have made such an impact or have had the initiative to write his Gospel without the encouragement from his cousin, Barnabas? Both Paul and Mark received *courage* from Barnabas.

The other exogenous act of empowerment that was mentioned in the verse above is the act of appointing elders. The spiritual DNA/Holy Spirit within the disciples can motivate them to do many amazing things. Over time disciples become so transformed by this endogenous power that they no longer resemble normal people. They become aliens and strangers in the world and relate more to the things of heaven than to earth. But there are things that they do not know inherently.

Unless they are instructed by more mature disciples, they will not know about baptism and why it is important for every disciple. They will not know what the Lord's Supper is and that the Lord commanded disciples to observe it. They will not know how to structure themselves, as a church, in accordance with biblical teaching. These are things that came through the teaching of the apostles and are now outlined for us in the Bible. A disciple could live without these things, just as a child could live without any instruction from his parents, but he would not mature properly and would not realize his potential.

Remember that the first three elements of church-planting movements are:

- Prayer
- Abundant Gospel sowing
- Intentional church planting

▶ **Ingredients**

Now take another look at the last seven elements and remember that each of these is related to number three: intentional church planting. The first four in the list are the methods by which an apostolic team structures the church, and the last three are the results if everything is done correctly.

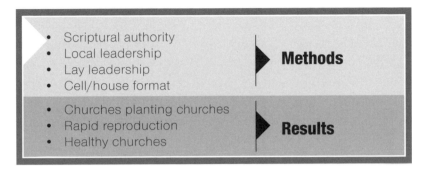

We have seen that an apostolic team empowers the church through encouragement and teaching. According to the research done on church-planting movements, some important practical areas of teaching are the first four issues listed above. The church must base everything on Scripture, have leadership that comes from its own community, not pay the leadership, and avoid institutionalization.

The last three elements are the expected results when everything is done correctly. The Holy Spirit motivates the church to multiply with such passion that multiplication is aggressive and dynamic. The Holy Spirit also instructs us to throw off everything that prevents us from knowing Christ and from living lives worthy of our calling as disciples. In this way the church purifies itself and is healthy. Disciples naturally fellowship and worship together, edify one another through teaching, and exhibit spiritual gifts. So, if the church is made up of authentic disciples and is structured according to biblical teachings, the church *will* be healthy and *will* multiply by starting other churches.

An apostolic team can facilitate the last three church-planting movement elements by encouraging those results directly. Although the Holy Spirit encourages these things, it is still good for the apostolic team to fight against the deceptions of Satan and to teach directly about churches planting churches, rapid reproduction, and healthy churches.

As a review, empowering the church involves entrusting the church to the Lord, encouraging the church, and educating the church. Another "E" of empowerment is *exiting*, as shown in this example: "So Paul, having stayed on for many days, said goodbye to the brothers and sailed away to Syria" (Acts 18:18a).

By *exiting* the community, the apostolic minister removes any seeming source of human help from the church. The church can no longer come to the apostolic team to solve its problems and is forced to depend upon the stronger endogenous power, the Holy Spirit. He is exceedingly faithful to us when we depend upon Him.

Although the incarnational work ends at this point, the church-planting component of *empowering the church* should continue. Paul, Peter, Jude, and John continued to write letters to encourage and instruct the churches, and the New Testament is full of examples of disciples being sent on short-term trips to empower the church through more encouragement, teaching, and structuring of the church. As we get into the next section of this book, I will also show you other ways in which volunteers can empower the church.

All of these ways of empowering the church result in disciples who are passionate about building the kingdom of God. They will pray earnestly for other communities or people groups who have yet to hear the Gospel, and they will make plans to reach them. The step of *empower the church* results in another cycle in which the newly-made disciples go out to *enter the community* in an unreached area. There they will *make disciples* and *empower the church* that they have begun in order to maintain and multiply the cycle.

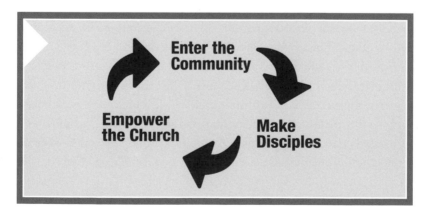

It's simple. Apostolic workers are sent out and enter into places where the Gospel has never been. The result of their disciple-making work is disciples. These disciples are super-human through the power of the Holy Spirit, and they gather as a church to become a great powerhouse for God. The strategy of this church is to equip every member and send them out to the community, neighboring communities, and nearby people groups. In this way the church expands multiplicatively, like a snowball rolling downhill, overcoming even the ancient barriers of Satan.

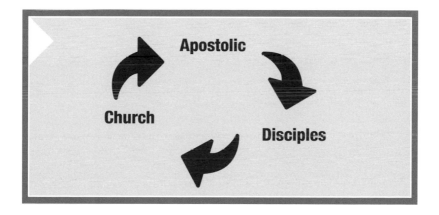

As a quick review, here are the three church-planting components again:

1. Enter the community; just follow the ABCs.
2 Make disciples, and get to it right away.
3. Empower the church, giving them everything that they need to multiply.

PART THREE
Health Strategy Possibilities

INTRODUCTION

The third section of this book, proposing health strategy possibilities, is another way that you can empower the church. By training national disciples in these strategies, you are creating practical ways to engage communities and other towns in a region. At this point, let us take a look at an overview of some of these health strategies. The objective here is not to explain all of the details but to cast a vision for possibilities. The best strategy may well be your own ideas or a mix of the examples.

At the beginning of the strategy, a three-star rating system evaluates strengths for *enter the community*, *make disciples*, and *empower the church*. In addition, whether the strategy is appropriate for a rural/urban setting or developing/developed nation will be indicated. It was difficult to determine which strategy fit best under which category because I have not seen all of these strategies being tried under all circumstances. For example, I have seen a family wellness strategy used successfully in rural settings but do not know of a church-planting team that has tried it in an urban setting. Therefore, some of the scoring is my best logical guess.

When *enter the community* receives a higher rating, the strategy is particularly favorable for an outside apostolic team, even of non-nationals, to get permissions and begin working in unreached areas. A strategy that receives a higher rating for *make disciples* is one in which numerous families are being visited and are receptive to the message of the disciple maker. These strategies address problems that are personal or important to families being served. The strategies receiving a higher rating for *empower the church* require less training and are implemented easily by national disciples so that they can make disciples, usually within a matter of weeks.

The chapter on "volunteers" explores an option that may be an important adjunct to many strategies. In fact, we have seen the use of volunteers move apostolic teams beyond barriers that had been thought impenetrable. As you read through the various health strategies, consider whether the use of volunteers could benefit your overall plan.

CHAPTER 9

THE LUKE 10 STRATEGY

Enter the Community	Make Disciples	Empower the Church
✪ ✪	✪ ✪ ✪	✪ ✪ ✪

✔ URBAN ✔ RURAL ✔ DEVELOPED ✔ DEVELOPING

The area had been closed to all Westerners for decades but was now forced to open its doors because of a humanitarian crisis. After several days of travel, we reached the largest city of the state where we set up a temporary base. Somehow we missed our contact at the airport. We were greeted, however, by a native of that country who had been sent to meet us. He hustled us into the back of a taxi and with the largest smile asked, "Are any of you pastors or evangelists?" We stated shyly that we were doctors and community development workers, which seemed to disappoint him. "I am an evangelist," he said. "The Lord has called me here to save these Muslim people."

The man who we were supposed to meet at the airport came on a later flight. He also considered himself to be an evangelist and church planter to this unreached part of his country.

We left the city, traveled to remote areas, and returned the next day. Upon our return, we were visited by a young man working for another humanitarian aid organization. As he was leaving, he surprised me and said, "Well, I must go, but remember me. My name is Ahmed, and I am here as a witness for the Lord Jesus Christ so I may share the Gospel with these people."

Prior to our visit, we were not aware of any evangelical witness for the 1 million people in that area, but within two nights, the Lord introduced us to three apostolic ministers. This is commonly the case. God is orchestrating a great work all around us to advance His kingdom to the ends of the earth. Just as we see in the book of Acts, God is doing more than we realize. He knows the future for all nations and has a plan to bring a remnant from each to repentance and faith in Jesus Christ.

So, let's talk strategy. In the above situation, what would you do to come alongside God and make the greatest impact against physical and spiritual darkness? Where would you begin and in which direction would you go?

THE PROBLEM

Apostolic ministers working among unreached people groups don't like the math confronting them. The number of people in their region with no access to the Gospel is often in the hundreds of thousands, and they are spread out over huge areas. Resources to reach the lost are usually comprised of a few team members and a few thousand dollars for projects. The amount of work to be done appears insurmountable.

Unreached people groups are unreached for good reasons. It has been almost 2,000 years since Jesus told us to make disciples of all nations, and 39 percent of humanity still has no access to the Gospel. This means that the vast majority of people within these populations will live entire lives without ever meeting a disciple of Jesus or hearing about the one pathway to salvation. Where that task of making disciples is easier, it has been accomplished already; today, most of the nations that are still unevangelized are hostile to the Gospel. In the above example, the government would expel any humanitarian organization from the country if it suspected that the humanitarian workers were trying to make disciples of Christ. Members of the community would persecute anyone who showed interest in Jesus.

THE STRATEGY

We disciples are a part of a body, and Jesus is the head. He is always in front of us, working in places before we even get there. In the example above, He already had sent other members of the body to the target area. Besides the three men, it is not known how many other apostolic workers had been called by God and were already in the region. He needs the body to come together so that they will have the synergy to accomplish His tasks. The national disciples are able to communicate the Gospel more clearly, so the task at hand is to empower them to make the greatest impact.

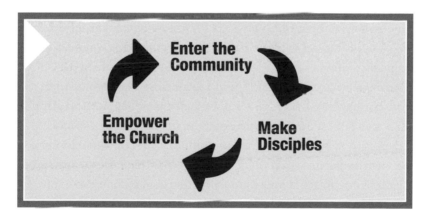

In this scenario, we are entering the church-planting cycle at *empower the church*. We do not need to concentrate on making disciples, because some disciples already are present. In fact, they have graduated from being disciples to being apostolic workers who have been sent out by the Lord to make more disciples. These men had stated that they were sent by the Lord to save the lost, so strategic thinking from this point should revolve around the question of how we can best enable these *sent ones* to be successful. They may not be from that area of the country, but they are still Christ's church, and they need to be trained to *enter the community*, *make disciples*, and *empower the church* that they establish.

This last section of the book will introduce many strategies. One could train and mobilize these disciple makers through a tuberculosis strategy, instruction about nutrition and hygiene, ministry with refugees, etc. Whether or not one of these strategies is used, all disciple makers should first be trained in the simple Luke 10 strategy. This is the purest form of *preach and heal* and was taught directly from Jesus to the first church. It is to be learned and practiced by every disciple and taught to everyone who is not already utilizing it. The other strategies that we will look at are really elaborations of this first strategy.

As an overview, take a look at all that Jesus taught in Luke 10:1-9:

> After this, the Lord appointed 70 others, and He sent them ahead of Him in pairs to every town and place where He Himself was about to go. He told them: "The harvest is abundant, but the workers are few. Therefore, pray to the Lord of the harvest to send out workers into His harvest. Now go; I'm sending you out like lambs among wolves. Don't carry a money-bag, traveling bag, or sandals; don't greet anyone along the road. Whatever house you enter, first say, 'Peace to this household.' If a son of peace is there, your peace will rest on him; but if not, it will return to you. Remain in the same house, eating and drinking what they offer, for the worker is worthy of his wages. Don't be moving from house to house. When you enter any town, and they welcome you, eat the things set before you. Heal the sick who are there, and tell them, 'The kingdom of God has come near you.'

THE RIGHT FOUNDATION

The Luke 10 strategy is very simple, but it is built completely upon a foundation of faith. Faith is required to leave one's comfort zone and "go." Faith is required to find a "man of peace." Mostly, faith is required to "heal the sick who are there."

Jesus was commanding these disciples to heal the sick by supernatural means. There is no evidence in the New Testament of healing occurring by medicine. Every instance of healing that is recorded is through the power of God. However, does this command to "heal" apply to us today? In Matthew 10, Jesus called His 12 disciples, gave them authority over evil spirits and illnesses, and sent them out. From that point on, His disciples are referred to as "the twelve apostles." On that occasion, though, Jesus not only told them to "heal the sick" but also to "raise the dead." Do both commands apply to us? Does one apply and the other not? Or does neither command apply? Are we to pray for the sick to be healed? Are we to pray for the dead to be raised and expect to see that in our ministry?

Obviously, these are the kinds of questions that have divided the church for centuries. Many godly disciples today believe that these commands were only for the disciples who were standing before Jesus, and there are no longer miracles or supernatural healings of any kind. Many also believe that miracles were done through the apostolic age, or perhaps until the canonization of the Bible, but are absent today. On the other hand, there are many godly disciples who believe that every command of Jesus given to His disciples applies to all disciples throughout time. The question can't be settled by taking a vote, and since it is an argument that is still around after 2,000 years, I feel confident in saying that no one can come up with an answer that will suit everyone.

The situation is complicated further by flamboyant men who seem to perform miraculous healings on television but then purvey teachings that aren't always consistent with Scripture. Are all of these healings authentic, and are these true healers of today? Or are these healings fabricated?

I do not presume to have the ultimate answer to these questions. I have had many patients come back to me after I had prayed for their healing and tell me that they had been healed, some in dramatic ways. I also have heard many remarkable stories of miraculous healings and, yes, even people being raised from the dead. In India I even met a disciple who claimed that he had been raised from the dead. It is very common for me to read letters and e-mails from reliable colleagues who reference healings.

For example, a doctor in my house church gave this story even while I was writing this chapter:

> God performed a healing miracle at our refugee clinic. Most of our patients have diabetes and high blood pressure and because of poverty and instability, their illnesses are difficult to control. "Nabil," one of my diabetic patients, came in for his regular monthly checkup and asked me to take a look at his toes. Since he is one of my few diabetics with well-controlled fasting blood sugars, I was surprised and dismayed to see that he had developed dry gangrene in three of his toes. This elderly man didn't realize the severity of the problem, and I couldn't tell him that most likely he was going to need amputation. I sent him home to do some Betadine soaks while I figured out what to do, thinking I'd need to find a surgeon. We prayed for him in clinic and at house church on Sunday.
>
> The next morning, I arrived early for clinic with a friend and clinic volunteer, and we sat out in the car talking. I saw Nabil go to the waiting room. I told my friend that I dreaded seeing his toes and that I was convicted that I needed more faith to pray for healing. I prayed out of obedience but didn't really expect much, because it's so rare that we see miraculous healings.
>
> We went up to clinic, had our staff prayer time, and began seeing patients. A few minutes later, one of our nurses came into my office and said, "Dr. Hannah, you have to come see this!" I went to the nurses' screening

room where Nabil had his feet bared and looked at his previously gangrenous toes to see no evidence of gangrene but instead, living tissue. The dead tissue was gone. His toes had been brought back to life. I could just see God laughing. Not at me, of course (even though I deserved it) but to joyfully restore my faith.

Another doctor friend sent an e-mail that detailed so many miracles that I cannot print them all here. But here are a few excerpts:

In a nearby people group, H and DJ, two men who came to believe primarily through short-wave radio and the Good Book, have been taking the Good News to their people. They ride horse carts to villages about 70 kilometers away from town every few weeks.

The distance is not the only obstacle faced. When word got out that they were telling the Good News, a local *halifa* (Sultan's representative) threw them in jail. Their friends brought them food and water, but the *halifa* wouldn't allow them to eat.

Then a truly amazing thing happened. Everything the *halifa* ate or drank, he began to vomit. After a day and a half of this, the *halifa* decided to let them out of jail. As soon as they were released, the *halifa's* vomiting stopped. After witnessing to him, he believed and told them that they could freely tell the Good News!

A couple of months ago, they were witnessing in a village whose well had almost gone dry. The people were skeptical of their message but asked them to pray that the well would produce more water. They said they would only pray if they could pray in the name of Jesus, and the people allowed them to pray.

They returned to the village a few weeks later to warm greetings and joyful faces. The well had begun to produce water in such abundance that they had no trouble watering their herds as well as those of other villages. The well had more water than ever, and they were prepared to believe. In the weeks after, H and DJ returned several times to teach.

Then last month, they were confronted by an angry man. He said what they had done was sorcery and magic and not from the power of Jesus. He said it was blasphemy to say that Jesus was God's Son and could have that kind of power.

As the man began to walk away, he realized he couldn't see. Two days later, DJ and H received a message from the man to help him, because he still couldn't see.

The blind man told DJ a dream he had about a man in white named Jesus who told him to ask DJ to pray for him to be able to see. When DJ heard this, he was a little frightened and said to him, "Why don't you let me take you to the doctor [meaning the doctor who wrote this], and he could pray for you. He has been a believer longer than I." The man told DJ that Jesus' instructions were very specific that DJ should be the one to pray for him.

So DJ and H prayed for him. He did not immediately see but the next day when he woke up, he could see!

Then lastly, a man who had a paralyzed leg and arm had been taken to our local hospital by DJ and our coworkers. He was not able to get medicine. Our coworkers, H and DJ, prayed over him. After several days, he was no better and went back to his village. He had a dream that he was lying on his mat, and our coworker came to him and again prayed in Jesus' name for him to get up and walk. In the dream, he got up and was able to walk without his cane. The same night, he woke up to go to the bathroom and after several steps, he realized he had left his mat without his cane and was walking normally! Since then, many have been asking how it is possible that he is able to walk.

Here is another example, given by a colleague in a prayer letter:

S.P. was sharing the Gospel with 45 mostly professional and all unsaved Bengalis in Calcutta. As he concluded the Bible study, a man brought a woman with terminal cancer to him.

"Will you pray for her to show that your God is more powerful than the gods of Hinduism?" he asked. Though S.P. was spiritually exhausted and powerless, he prayed for her healing.

"When the prayer ended," he told me, "I fled for home on my motorcycle. I cried out to God to forgive me for the spiritual vacuum, the emptiness I felt. I was certain my prayer would go unanswered, and the men would not return the next week."

S.P. actually waited two weeks before he got up the courage to go back to the Bible study. When he did, he was amazed that all 45 were there including the "terminally ill" woman, now completely healed! He also found that 43 of the 45 Bengalis had accepted Christ even without him being present. More than a dozen new house churches have been started in the Bengali community as a result of this one miracle.

So these are some examples from the Middle East, Northern Africa, and India that I have run across. Events that seem unbelievable to Western minds are often expected, and reportedly seen, in Africa, China, India, and in other places in the East. At the same time, I can't say, as a scientist, that I have ever seen anything resembling the raising of the dead or anyone being miraculously healed immediately before my eyes. In my experience, God seems to work in the gray zone, often doing the miraculous but keeping His works somewhat obscure so that many never see what He is doing. Or, like Thomas, they cannot believe in things until they see and touch the miracle itself.

Keeping the complexities of this question in mind, I would recommend the following approach, regardless of the teachings that you have received by others and regardless of your personal bias. When I get stuck on a tough question, I always imagine myself standing at the judgment seat of Christ finding that I had been wrong.

If I had spent my life stubbornly believing that there were no modern-day miracles but found myself to be wrong, how would I feel? If Jesus asked me, "Charles, why did you never obey my command to use the power of the Holy Spirit to heal?" what would I answer? Although Jesus will completely forgive me, I will still be ashamed. To find that I had disobeyed Jesus would bring me much grief.

On the other hand, if I spent my life stubbornly believing that supernatural healings were a possibility and prayed for Christ's healings on many occasions, how would I feel at the judgment seat if I were wrong? Jesus would say something like, "Charles, my commands to heal were only for the disciples of that day. Why did you pray for the power of the Holy Spirit to heal in your day?"

In this situation, I also would be wrong, but at least I wouldn't be as ashamed. After all, even though my faith would have been ill-placed, my behavior still would have come from faith rather than from an intellectual decision or skepticism. In the first situation, I would be guilty of disobedience but in the second situation, I would only be guilty of being wrong, something that I am more comfortable with as my age advances. At my judgment, I expect to find that I was wrong about many things. During this life, though, I endeavor to live in such a way that the judgment will reveal fewer instances in which I had been disobedient.

By the way, this philosophical method is very similar to Blaise Pascal's famous argument. *Pascal's Gambit* argues that there are two possible positions on the questionable existence of God and two possible answers to the question. On the one hand, we can choose to believe in God or choose not to believe in God. Ultimately, we can end up being right, or we can end up being wrong. Pascal came to the logical conclusion that it is wisest to believe in the existence of God.

	God Exists	God Does Not Exist
Belief in God	Go To Heaven	Nothing After Death
No Belief in God	Go To Hell	Nothing After Death

The question about miracles also can be put into a similar table resulting in a similar conclusion. The two boxes with the lighter shading are the two possibilities where I turned out to be wrong.

	Miracles Exist	Miracles Do Not Exist
I Pray for Miracles	God's response is, "Well done."	God's response is, "You were wrong."
I Do Not Pray for Miracles	God's response is, "You disobeyed Me."	God's response is, "You were right."

My recommendation for those who can accept it is to maintain an open and humble position. If you stick to the belief that miracles no longer occur, and you get to heaven and find out that you were right, big deal. You aren't going to impress God with the stuff in which you were right. You are going to please Him in those areas in which you were obedient.

We are going to make mistakes, so lean in your behavior so that your mistakes will make the least offense to Jesus. I suggest that even the most skeptical disciple should adjust his behavior to pray for healings. In addition to adjusting your behavior, adjust your expectations. Expect, in faith, for the Holy Spirit to act and to heal. This faith is essential as Scripture explicitly says, "The prayer of faith will save the sick person, and the Lord will raise him up" (James 5:15a).

THE STEPS OF A LUKE 10 STRATEGY

The Luke 10 strategy is very simple. One need only follow the directives given by Jesus: "After this, the Lord appointed 70 others, and He sent them ahead of Him in pairs to every town and place where He Himself was about to go" (Luke 10:1).

The first step is to pair disciples so that no one is working alone. Jesus sent disciples out in pairs of two. Twice as many towns could have been reached by sending out single disciples, so why did Jesus do this?

In my own experience and from talking to many colleagues on this subject, the benefits of having ministry partners greatly outweigh the setbacks. The primary advantage is the synergy attained from joining two disciples together. My understanding of synergy came from my study of pharmacology, and I have found it very applicable in ministry.

To test the effectiveness of an antibiotic, scientists take a tiny disk of cardboard, soak it in a solution made from an antibiotic, and then lay it onto a dish full of bacteria. After a time, they look at the dish and measure the clear zone around the disk where the antibiotic has killed the germs.

A good antibiotic may kill all of the germs around the disk, creating a circle of dead germs measuring one centimeter. Another antibiotic disk can be placed in a similar dish, and it may create a zone of dead germs also measuring one centimeter. Synergy between the two antibiotics, however, is demonstrated when a disk is saturated with both antibiotics. For the two antibiotics to be declared *synergistic*, they must be able to kill a greater area of germs than either could do on their own. In some cases, two drugs, such as described, can be added together to create a zone of dead germs measuring 1.5 centimeters. This is a greater area than a scientist would expect and is very important as there may be no other single drug that can create such an effect.

At first it appears that this is an argument against apostolic partnerships. In the analogy, each antibiotic disk was killing a one centimeter circle each. Counting both disks, two centimeter circles worth of germs were killed. When they were combined, only a 1.5 centimeter circle had been killed, which is less. Look at the last sentence of the previous paragraph. By joining the two antibiotics, they were able to kill germs that had been resistant to every other single antibiotic. So synergy gives the power to do something, as a pair or group, which cannot be done by agents acting on their own. Many people groups are still unevangelized even though apostolic ministers have tried to make an impact among them. Just like an antibiotic, they are *resistant* to the effects of a single apostolic worker. Through the power of synergistic partnerships, though, it is possible that a team could make disciples among one of these many unreached and resistant areas.

In addition to *synergy*, there are some practical reasons why it is wise to do ministry with a partner. I cannot tell you how many times I have been explaining the Gospel, perhaps doing well for an hour, but at the part about the crucifixion of Jesus, interruptions start, such as a visitor coming in, the baby waking up, a phone call, etc. If one has a wise partner, he can immediately handle these interruptions so that the speaker can continue with the Gospel. When there are no interruptions, the non-speaking partner can be praying.

The first step in the Luke 10 strategy is to put disciples into disciple-making teams of two. It is the smart thing to do; it was done by the disciples before and after their time with Jesus, and this is the method that Jesus taught.

The second step is prayer: "The harvest is abundant, but the workers are few. Therefore, pray to the Lord of the harvest to send out workers into His harvest" (Luke 10:2). Take another look at the verses from Luke 10 and see how Jesus told the disciples to pray and specifically ask for more laborers. This point is especially pertinent when considering the vast regions that I have mentioned that are as yet unreached with the Gospel. More laborers are desperately needed if we are to extend the message of salvation to the ends of the earth and if you are to reach all of the communities in your target area.

When we look at the New Testament, we see that these laborers come from two places. A minority came from the core group of disciples that Jesus chose in Capernaum. The majority of laborers came from the new disciples who had been made in distant lands as they traveled.

As has been said, we have the most information about Paul's ministry, and the New Testament mentions dozens of men who worked as laborers with him. Barnabas, Silas, John Mark, and perhaps a few others came from the core group in Jerusalem or Antioch. But Timothy, Aquila and Priscilla, Sopater, Aristarchus, Secundus, Gaius, Titus, Epaphroditus, Onesimus, Tychicus, Justus, Epaphras, Erastus, Trophimus, Artemus, and many others are mentioned as working with Paul and were products of his disciple-making ministry. The majority of laborers are in the harvest.

Therefore, the second step is to teach your disciple-making teams to pray not only that the Lord will make disciples where they go, but that these will be authentic disciples who will become co-laborers to spread the Gospel.

The third step is to teach the disciple-making teams how to *enter the community*: "Now go; I'm sending you out like lambs among wolves. Don't carry a money-bag, traveling bag, or sandals; don't greet anyone along the road" (Luke 10:3-4). The direction from Jesus was simply to "Go!" Yet, He also taught them to expect danger, to depend upon their faith for the supply of their needs, and not to be distracted. These same issues should be taught to the disciple-making teams that you train. Your trainees already may be living in the unreached target area. If this is the case, teach them what Jesus taught about *going*.

The fourth step in the Luke 10 strategy is to find the "man of peace." "Whatever house you enter, first say, 'Peace to this household.' If a son of peace is there, your peace will rest on him; but if not, it will return to you. Remain in the same house, eating and drinking what they offer, for the worker is worthy of his wages. Don't be moving from house to house. When you enter any town, and they welcome you, eat the things set before you" (Luke 10:5-8). This issue was discussed in Chapter Six. Explain to your disciple-making teams the characteristics of a "man of peace," and teach them to expect this divine appointment. If you are working in a culture that does not have the custom of having travelers stay in local homes, teach your disciple-making teams to find lodging elsewhere, find a person of peace, and spend as much time with that person as possible. He will guide the team to ministry opportunities.

Have the teams look for signs of illness everywhere they go, and ask the person of peace to identify the sick. As soon as there is a report of an illness, they should ask for permission to make a visit. When appropriate, have the person of peace accompany the team to the sick person's house and make introductions.

The fifth step is to heal the sick: "Heal the sick who are there" (Luke 10:9a). Have the disciple-making team bring a gift of flowers, fruit, soda, etc., to the sick person. Teach them to enter into homes humbly and as servants to the family.

Don't forget the basics: you entered this house to preach and to heal.

A sick person loves to talk about his illness, and he frequently feels as if he has not been heard. Have the disciple makers ask a question about the patient's overall state and listen. The team should demonstrate concern by asking questions about the illness. They can ask how long it has been going on, what the patient has tried in the past for relief, what the doctor said, if he was able to get the right medicines, if he has benefited from the medicines, how this problem is affecting the family, etc. Being able to voice his misery will make the sick person feel better. You may want to teach the team how to feel a patient's forehead for fever or how to check a pulse, but no medical treatment needs to be made.

After a long visit, have the team ask for permission to pray for the patient. If this is granted, then they should pray that the person would be healed. There is no magic prayer formula. The point is to acknowledge that Jesus is greater than any illness and to ask Him to bring healing. James 5:14 instructs us to anoint the sick with oil, a directive which I recommend.

Remember that this may be the first time that the team is showing themselves as disciples of Jesus. They should already have shared this with the person of peace, but now they are telling others who may not be on their side. The breach must be crossed or else the name of Jesus will go unspoken, and God will not have an opportunity to show His power. This must be done in faith, on the first visit, demonstrating that the reason they came was to bring healing through the name of Jesus. You do not want them to think that it has just been a social visit. After prayer, have the teams ask for permission to come back the next day. Upon return, have them bring another gift.

If there is no apparent healing, teach the disciples that there is no need to make an excuse for Jesus. He is perfectly capable of defending His own honor and does it in His own way. When Paul prayed for self-healing, he was not healed, but the Lord spoke to him in a way that was more useful than a healing (2 Corinthians 12:7-9).

The Luke 10 strategy was given before the church existed or salvation through the blood of Jesus was available. The statement, ". . . and tell them, 'The kingdom of God has come near you'" (Luke 10:9b) was the Gospel at that time. When we follow this strategy today, we are able to give the complete Gospel—the kingdom of God has now come, and Jesus is the doorway to that kingdom. Through this message, disciples are made, which is the sixth step in the strategy. The last step for the disciple-making team is to gather these disciples into groups and, among other things, to teach them the Luke 10 strategy.

Steps in a *Luke 10* strategy

1. Create disciple-making teams of two disciples per team
2. Pray for more laborers
3. Enter the community
4. Find the *man of peace*
5. Heal the sick that are there

6. Make disciples
7. Empower the church

 Post-resurrection interpretation of "... tell them, 'The Kingdom of God has come near to you.'"

IMPLICATIONS FOR A
CHURCH-PLANTING MOVEMENT

As you can see, this strategy meets all of the requirements of the health strategy ABCs. If used correctly, it can give apostles and disciples direct access into even hostile places where the Gospel has never been before. It effectively gets behind closed doors. It cares for the needy. And because it allows for multiple visits behind closed doors, it provides an excellent platform for making disciples and empowering those disciples as a church.

Remember, it is not the power of medical skills that brings people to Christ. Nor is it the power of persuasive argument. None of the disciples that Jesus chose went to medical school or seminary. They were neither preachers nor healers. The skills taught in those institutions are not necessary, and may even be detrimental, to being an effective instrument for the Lord. In 1 Corinthians 2:1-5, Paul wrote:

> When I came to you, brothers, announcing the testimony of God to you, I did not come with brilliance of speech or wisdom. For I determined to know nothing among you except Jesus Christ and Him crucified. And I was with you in weakness, in fear, and in much trembling. My speech and my proclamation were not with persuasive words of wisdom, but with a demonstration of the Spirit and power, so that your faith might not be based on men's wisdom but on God's power.

The Luke 10 strategy gives nationals an opportunity to demonstrate compassion to the lost, but its greatest strength is that it provides an opportunity for God to demonstrate His power. There are other disciple-making strategies, but the Luke 10 strategy should be added to whatever else you are doing. I encourage you to step out in faith and utilize the very strategy that Jesus gave us.

CHAPTER 10

VOLUNTEERS

Enter the Community	Make Disciples	Empower the Church
⭐ ⭐	⭐ ⭐ ⭐	⭐ ⭐ ⭐

✅ URBAN ✅ RURAL ✅ DEVELOPED ✅ DEVELOPING

The war had lasted longer than expected with guerilla fighting continuing throughout the country. Apostolic workers excitedly had moved in, but the security situation was preventing much real work. Because of the conflict, internally displaced persons were everywhere, and we visited them to determine their needs. It was winter, and dozens of families had built partitions of mud bricks and aluminum under the town's soccer stadium bleachers. They huddled in the cold needing everything.

The long-term worker did his best to buy blankets, mittens, heaters, and a little food, but he was only one guy to help with never ending needs. We had seen many children needing medical care, so we requested teams of doctors and dentists to come from the U.S. A few teams were interested until they heard the name of the target country, which was seen on TV each night. They all dropped out but one.

A doctor from a church in North Carolina never wavered as he put together a team of volunteers, collected his medicines, and bought their flight tickets. The first question that every other team had asked had been in regard to safety, but Dr. Rich never asked that question. We had told him about the physical and spiritual needs, we had explained the strategy, and we had told him that we would do everything that we could to keep the team safe. That was good enough for them. They moved forward relentlessly, despite warnings from friends and family, working on a very tight schedule.

They were actually in the country for only one week but were able to provide free medical clinics for the refugees for five days. They performed admirably, demonstrating great compassion and praying for many patients. However, after the team left, the security situation worsened, and even the long-term worker left the area. It seemed as if all had been for naught. All of the planning, all of the work, even the short-term clinic was left with no follow up. The vision grew dark.

Six months later, I was asked to visit a town far in the north of the country. I flew into the capital, took a second flight to the base town, and met a driver who was to take me to my destination. The temperature was 115 degrees, and the car had no air conditioning for the three-hour drive.

Hal, the young driver, asked me why I had come so far. I explained that I was a disciple of Jesus sent to care for the poor in that country. With sparkling eyes and a beautiful smile, he said, "I am a disciple of Jesus also. A medical team from America came here, and one of the members led me to Jesus on March 3. The leader of the team was Dr. Rich. They were amazing servants to the people. They even gathered to pray for the Muslims right in front of them."

For three hours we talked about our lives in Christ. The meeting in the north was a waste of time, but Hal and I talked about Jesus for another three hours on the way home. Because of security reasons, we had to avoid some towns and Hal got lost on three occasions. Each time, when he asked for directions, he gave JESUSfilms and literature to the Muslims who had helped us. "Please look at this," he said. "Jesus has changed my life."

Eighteen months passed before I saw Hal again. This time, he told me about the small house church that he had started in a nearby *town. The vision had been passed to another disciple, and the Christ within him, which shone through his eyes and echoed through his words, became the hope of glory for the people of that area. It started with one faithful worker and a volunteer team from North Carolina that answered "yes."*

We are living in a time like no other. There is an unprecedented ease of travel, communication, affluence, and number of evangelical disciples. As a result, there are more short-term apostolic volunteers than at any time in history. "Short-term missions," in quotes, results in over 250,000 hits on Google. Nevertheless, not all volunteer teams are a benefit to church-planting strategy; some are detrimental.

The bad experiences result from a variety of reasons and may be avoided by following some core values. Some of these put the responsibility on the short-term volunteers; some put responsibility on the long-term workers.

CORE VALUES FOR SHORT-TERM APOSTOLIC TEAMS

I am continually asked the question, "My friend isn't a Christian, but can I bring him on this short-term trip? I think it will be good for him." There is no denying that lives have been changed by a short-term mission trip. In fact, the primary reason for the trips for many churches is to change the volunteers, resulting in increased giving for missions and perhaps leading some church members to become apostolic workers.

However, changing the lives of people in the Western church is not the reason for short-term missions. The reason for all apostolic work, short- and long-term, is to make disciples and establish a healthy church in a previously unreached community. Non-disciples are not able to help in this purpose and are likely to send the wrong message to nationals. An authentic disciple is decidedly different from other humans, and an important purpose of short-term teams is to model that difference. When volunteer teams return to their home country, we often hear reports of how loving and selfless each visitor had been. Only one non-disciple on the team, behaving in a worldly way, can destroy that reputation.

This is not to say that these disciples will not undergo considerable spiritual growth on these trips. My life is continually being changed as I reach out to a lost world, and it is only natural for all short-term workers to have the same experience. They will give financially to apostolic work, and many of them will leave their homes to become long-term workers. These are side benefits of mission trips but not the goal.

Many chapters ago we talked about three ingredients found in church-planting movements: prayer, abundant Gospel sowing, and intentional church planting. A visiting team needs to get the most out of a short time. So, the most bang for the buck is through prayer. It is best for a team to have other specific church-planting objectives, but before, during, and after work, volunteers should be in constant prayer for the area in which they are serving.

Long-term apostolic life breaks down into three categories: survival, maintenance, and productivity. At times, survival and family maintenance take up 100 percent of our time. Repairing something broken, finding and preparing food, waiting in offices and filling out forms to appease the government, and educating children take time. Our goal is to get those things done quickly, ignore some of those that are just related to comfort, and maximize the time spent in productive activities. Disciples cannot be made if we simply make a life for ourselves in foreign communities.

So, the last thing that is needed is for volunteer teams to increase the workload of their hosts. Of course they will need housing, food, water, and other things that they cannot get on their own, but the burden that they place on the apostolic families should be kept to a minimum.

They must also maintain the perspective that they are short-term visitors. The national disciples and the apostolic workers are the leaders in the area, and short-term workers learn from them, must defer to them, and must submit in all ways to their authority.

Related to this, short-term workers must think of themselves as servants. Short-term medical teams were asked to go into a restricted country that had just been through war. The volunteers were American, and the war had been against American-backed troops. Consequently, the American volunteers were harassed and challenged by many nationals. The teams stated honestly that Jesus had sent them to care for the needs of those who had been through the war. Immediately all barriers were broken down; they helped many people, opportunities to share their faith developed, and many gave their lives to Christ. To think of themselves primarily as Americans would have been seriously detrimental to the work.

Concerning work, short-term teams must do something that the apostolic workers cannot do for themselves. Before teams arrive, they should communicate frequently with the long-term workers to determine exactly what needs to be done. They can make suggestions based upon their areas of expertise, and should work out a plan so that the apostolic worker will accomplish something that would otherwise be too time consuming, too expensive, or impossible without outside help. This plan should be written as a list of objectives that move the apostolic team closer to the goal of establishing reproducing churches.

Core values for short-term apostolic teams

Volunteer apostolic teams:
1. Only bring authentic disciples
2. Are known by their prayer
3. Are not burdensome to their hosts
4. Treat national disciples and apostolic workers as their leaders
5. Are servants, surrendering any personal agenda
6. Do something for the apostolic workers that workers cannot do for themselves
7. Achieve objectives that move the apostolic team closer to church planting

POSSIBLE ACTIVITIES FOR VOLUNTEER TEAMS

The work of volunteer teams will vary depending upon the health strategy being utilized. In a very restricted Muslim country, an apostolic worker had made many disciples so that a church of more than 20 adults was gathering regularly. We sent short-term mobile medical teams to them, one in spring and one in autumn. When I next met with these disciples, they asked me to send more medical teams because they helped these national disciples gain access into communities where they needed some kind of an introduction. "We could use 10 of these teams every year," they told me.

These clinical teams are made up of doctors, dentists, and/or optometrists, and they provide free or cheap medical services to the needy. They bring their own medicines, or buy them locally, and ordinarily give these away also. They have great logistical needs, such as permissions from authorities and local doctors, housing, a place to operate their clinic, translators, etc. But they can be a wonderful boost to many strategies.

In another Muslim country, a church-planting team of national disciples wanted to establish a church among another people group in a city with no known disciples. They visited the area regularly for five years but never had any converts. They then asked for a volunteer medical team of one doctor, a nurse practitioner, a nurse who ran registration and a nursing desk, and two more that helped in the pharmacy and did odd tasks. The entire team worked very long hours and demonstrated a great amount of love for the people. After the team left, the church-planting team continued visiting where they had seen no converts in the past, and saw three families come to Christ almost immediately. One man asked for a JESUSfilm and showed it at his house over several months. After the next volunteer medical team came, over nine large families had come to faith in Jesus.

Besides clinical teams, we frequently send academic teams. These are usually teaching doctors or nurses who help an apostolic team gain credibility in a new setting or who support strategies in hospice, rehab, tuberculosis, HIV/AIDS, psychological counseling, or birth-attendant training. These experts can teach local health workers, but it is more helpful if they train national disciples and apostolic workers.

Disaster relief volunteers can provide medical services or can help out in a number of ways. They can train disciple makers in counseling, provide expertise in securing safe water and waste management, or run a food kitchen. Engineers and construction experts can help out after an earthquake, or volunteers can do research for community development teams. Since they don't speak the language, they must be accompanied by national disciple makers. They can have a great time together praying over unreached communities, studying the needs of the community, and sharing the Gospel after the work has been done.

Kinds of volunteer teams

1. Clinical
2. Academic
3. Disaster relief
4. Construction
5. Community development research

CONCLUSION

Some apostolic workers do not like short-term volunteers. With poor planning, volunteer teams actually can be a hindrance to the work. Volunteers may go home frustrated, feeling like missionaries don't really do anything, and apostolic workers may have to spend hours in repentant prayer because of their thoughts about a volunteer.

But, by following some simple core values, volunteer teams can be a decisive benefit and can give a church-planting strategy a great boost. Christ-centered volunteers must come and prepare themselves for physical and spiritual difficulties. At the same time, in addition to working out all of the logistics, the apostolic workers must clearly define the church-planting objectives that they want volunteers to achieve and must position the volunteers appropriately.

When it all comes together, it is a thing of beauty. The national disciples are delighted to meet brothers and sisters from far away and frequently say what an encouragement it is to know that there are other disciples out there. The volunteers work hard and are thrilled to do it for their Lord. The apostolic worker coordinates the project so that this three-part church comes together to advance the Gospel even further into enemy territory.

CHAPTER 11

HOSPICE

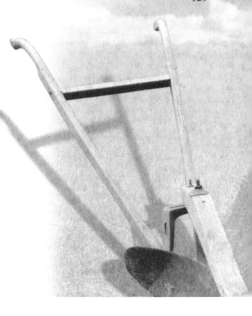

Enter the Community ✪ ✪   **Make Disciples** ✪ ✪ ✪   **Empower the Church** ✪ ✪ ✪

✔URBAN   ✔RURAL   ✔DEVELOPED   ✔DEVELOPING

Hospice: *a program of medical and emotional care for the seriously ill*
Palliation: *easing the severity of pain or a disease without removing the cause*

THE PROBLEM

In the old days, as a person was seriously ill or dying, the doctor and nurse had few treatment options available and spent considerable time sitting at the patient's side. They provided support mainly through palliative care, doing their best to relieve symptoms and give encouragement. As the field of medicine has advanced, however, the attention of these care professionals has largely shifted from the bedside to science. After all, medical management of each patient is extremely complex and requires attention.

To fill the bedside gap, clever people—probably nurses—came up with ideas such as *hospice*. The term hospice refers to support-ive services for the terminally ill. But these services are very rare in most African and Eastern countries. Doctors are seen at offices or at hospitals, but once a family walks out the door, that family is on its own. When a patient is unable to rest because of pain, is depressed because of loss of function, is worsening more rapidly because of lack of exercise and proper nutrition, and a family is at their wits end from living with such a heavy burden, there is no one to call for help.

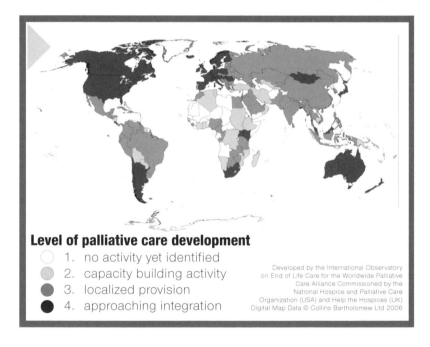

Level of palliative care development
1. no activity yet identified
2. capacity building activity
3. localized provision
4. approaching integration

Developed by the International Observatory on End of Life Care for the Worldwide Palliative Care Alliance Commissioned by the National Hospice and Palliative Care Organization (USA) and Help the Hospices (UK) Digital Map Data © Collins Bartholomew Ltd 2006

THE STRATEGY

Ordinarily, hospice is reserved only for the terminally ill who have less than six months to live. For our purposes, the principles of hospice can be applied to patients who are dying or who suffer with chronic disease. There are two reasons why it is preferable to expand the definition of hospice in this way.

First, the issue of dying is not commonly discussed in many cultures. When I was in residency, I did a rotation in the country of Thailand. One night, a family brought in their son who had a gunshot wound to the head. It was obvious to us that the patient would not survive long, but the family had been told by physicians at another hospital to admit him, and he would be fine. This is standard practice for most doctors in many cultures. Commonly, it is felt to be best for the patient to not know about their terminal condition, and sometimes the truth is even kept from the family. Since it is often culturally inappropriate to define a population as being terminally ill, we must adjust the definition of hospice so that we can cater to those who need hospice care, even though we may not know if they are just seriously ill or are in their last weeks of life.

Second, our objective is to get into as many homes as possible to care for hurting families. By expanding our definition of hospice, we are able to care for patients who are old, who have serious diseases such as tuberculosis, or who have severe chronic diseases such as rheumatoid arthritis.

As in all strategies, the hospice strategy is best when used to *empower the church*. The idea should be presented to disciples who are interested in becoming competent in the basics of hospice care as a means to reach their region. If no disciples are present, the strategy can also be used by an apostolic team coming from outside of the community.

A hospice strategy can be modified in many ways to fit your needs. At its simplest form, it can be a variation of the Luke 10 strategy. As disciples or the apostolic team are visiting the sick, they can pay particular attention to *hospice patients* who have not responded to prayers for healing and who are particularly in need. Initially these persons can be visited for several consecutive days and a schedule set up for regular visits, perhaps twice each week. As opposed to the Luke 10 strategy, however, this strategy entails teaching about health, which we will get into later. Another idea to consider is to have a nurse visit with the hospice team for an evaluation and recommendations. This nurse easily can be hired for these services, and it sends a very positive message to the hurting family when they see that disciples have gone to their own expense to get professional care for their family member.

Taking the strategy a step further, one could advertise these hospice services so as to find extremely ill people throughout a community or city. Producing a brochure of your work for local doctors gives opportunity to ask them to refer appropriate patients to your services. Explain that these services are to complement their work rather than compete. This would require some form of registration or license and could be done on three different levels: charity, not for profit, and for profit.

With the charity model, the hospice team uses team money and donations to pay for everything. They give of their time, they bring in a nurse, and they even bring in gifts and food, all at their own expense. If this charity is being advertised to the public, the nurse is necessary, and it may even be wise to have a doctor available for any questions. The doctor's name can be added to the brochure as the medical sponsor for the program, giving your team credibility and legal coverage and giving him free advertising.

The not-for-profit and for-profit models are more professional and do require medical backup through a local doctor. In both of these models, a qualified medical practitioner must do an in-home evaluation and some degree of money is charged. In the not-for-profit model, the charges cover the hospice team's expenses such as transportation, cell phones, food, or equipment. They also can cover possible salaries. All money made must be put back into the ministry. I only mention the for-profit model, because these businesses are sometimes easier to register. In this model, there is less accountability of money, and any profits could be used to fund other ministries.

Let me assure you again that health strategies do not require medical training. In fact, after a few hours of Internet research, you will know significantly more than a doctor or nurse about hospice care. Areas to be studied and services to be provided are:

1. Good nutrition and exercise
2. Nonmedical management of pain
3. Side effects of medicines and chemotherapy
4. Managing a bedridden patient
5. Spiritual counseling
6. Family counseling
7. Issues related to terminal illness

THE VISION AND CORE VALUES

Whether your program is an informal extension of the Luke 10 strategy, a professional business, or somewhere in the middle, it is helpful to develop a vision statement and a list of core values for your hospice team. Pretend to take a look into the future and assume that God has made your team completely successful. Now talk together about what you envisioned. Did you see families who had been cared for during the hardest times in their lives? Did you see new disciples? Did you see new churches using the hospice strategy to reach your entire city for Jesus? Work together to come up with a short vision statement that captures the essence of what you imagined.

Our hospice program's vision statement:

We envision hurting people and families being cared for, becoming disciples, and coming together into multiplying churches.

Core values are something like a constitution. They are a list of guidelines that all team members agree to work by. Here are some possible core values for a hospice strategy:

We provide quality care. It is very common for one to advise green tea for abdominal pain, cinnamon incense for nasal congestion, or red socks for headache because grandmother taught these things. But it is counterproductive and damaging to a team's credibility for them to make statements about treatment if they have no medical background. A team should only pass on information that they have learned about hospice care and completely avoid making medical diagnoses or treatment recommendations. Your team will not be able to handle many problems or answer many questions, but the care that you do give will be of good quality.

We are servants to needy people. Hospice workers are servants who have come to offer themselves to hurting patients and their families. We must be humble at all times and readily change dirty bandages, lift heavy patients, and help clean up.

We care about the whole person. As disciples and apostolic workers of Jesus Christ, we are trying to set ourselves apart from others whom the patient and family will encounter. Our objective is for them to be shocked by the depth of our compassion and, consequently, be eager to hear about the hope and peace within us. Therefore, we do not care just for the physical problems of our patients but also for their emotional, social, financial, and spiritual needs.

We work with your doctor to care for you in your home. It can be very damaging to your reputation if you are seen to be in competition with local healthcare workers. Therefore, you must meet with them to explain what you are doing and ask their advice on how your team can best serve these hurting families in their homes.

We keep all information confidential. I cannot overstate the importance of this point. It is morally wrong for you to reveal something you learned in a patient's home. These families are allowing you access to their secrets, and you cannot betray their confidence in you and your program. Everything that you learn, including the names of the families that you visit, must be kept in strictest confidence.

The core values of a hospice strategy

1. We provide quality care.
2. We are servants to needy people.
3. We care about the whole person.
4. We work with your doctor to care for you in your home.
5. We keep all information confidential.

IMPLICATIONS FOR A
CHURCH-PLANTING MOVEMENT

The longer I live, the more I realize that pride is the primary factor separating people from faith in Christ. A hard heart is just like rocky ground with no soil, so that it cannot accept the seed of the Gospel that is spread upon it. Yet, pride is weakest in the face of suffering. Think of the example of Paul's "thorn" in his flesh. He stated, specifically, that God had sent this messenger from Satan to prevent him from becoming conceited (2 Corinthians 12:7-9). Pain, whether physical or emotional, weakens the conceit of humankind, which is often necessary for the Gospel to penetrate into the heart of the lost.

Tragically, in every population, there is a significant percentage of people suffering from physical disease. This pain commonly causes people to become more withdrawn, depressed, and isolated from their neighbors because of the burden that they carry. The only good that could come from this suffering is that they are vulnerable to the Holy Spirit.

We are vessels of the Great Physician who have the capacity to soothe physical woes and introduce spiritual salvation. Even in the most restricted countries, little is preventing us from entering the homes of these suffering ones, caring for them in the name of Jesus, and telling them about His love. In the early centuries of Christianity, disciples became famous by caring for patients of leprosy, and this greatly benefited the spread of the Gospel. In this day, the same strategy is available through hospice care. Wouldn't it be wonderful to hear, as I have often heard, new disciples even giving thanks to God for their suffering because it was the means to their salvation?

CHAPTER 12

REHABILITATION

Enter the Community	Make Disciples	Empower the Church
✪ ✪ ✪	✪ ✪ ✪	✪ ✪

✔URBAN ✔RURAL ✔DEVELOPED ✔DEVELOPING

"Excuse me, doctor. Could you come with me for a minute?" my dinner host whispered in my ear as he helped lift me from the floor and my meal. I had just met this new friend a few days before, and he graciously invited several of us to his house for a traditional dinner with him and his three sons. His wife and daughters ate in another room.

We left the visitor's room and moved through dark corridors to the back of the house. In another room behind a curtain, an older woman sat by a boy in bed. The child was older than 10, had contractures of all limbs, and could not speak except to make unintelligible sounds. He fought as his grandmother tried to feed him and made bizarre faces and sounds.

"He is my son," my host said. "He has been like this since birth, and the doctors have not been able to help him. Is there anything that you can do?"

At first I did not understand. He had told me that he had three sons and all of them were now at the dinner table. I realized that this was another son that they did not count in public because of his profound disability. Because of their belief system, they related maladies such as this with some kind of wrongdoing or sin. To openly reveal the status of this child would be to reveal the family sin.

It was obvious that I could do nothing for the child, but it was equally obvious that much could be done to increase the range of motion of his limbs and to help the family care for him. Of course, that kind of help would have required some form of rehabilitative services and nothing like that was available in that large city.

THE PROBLEM

It is well-known by pediatricians that 6 percent of all children worldwide are born with a serious birth defect. That percentage is even higher in developing countries and in those places where consanguineous marriages (marriages between blood relatives) are common. At the same time, in those places with a higher incidence of birth defects, a profoundly decreased number of practitioners or agencies are available to help these patients.

Similarly, people who have had a serious accident, paralysis, or stroke are also in need of the rehabilitative services that are uncommon in Africa and Eastern countries. Special education teachers and physical, speech, and occupational therapists are difficult to find outside of the West, and in-home rehabilitative services are virtually nonexistent.

THE STRATEGY

A good definition of *rehabilitation* is "restoration to useful life through education and therapy." The rehabilitation strategy is almost identical to the hospice strategy except for this point about therapy. Whereas the hospice strategy does deal with counseling and education, it does not involve hands-on therapeutic care. The rehabilitation strategy, on the other hand, is very hands-on. This characteristic is both a strength and weakness of the strategy.

Unlike the hospice strategy in which information about nutrition and nonmedical pain management can be learned easily, the therapies for rehab patients vary greatly depending upon the disability. The term *rehabilitation* is extremely broad and covers everything from teaching someone in a leg cast how to use crutches to helping a child who has a profound mental impairment. A rehabilitation strategy requires at least one rehab practitioner for purposes of evaluation. It also requires that the rehab team be taught the kinds of services they are to provide. For this reason, the rehabilitation strategy is an exception among health strategies and could also be categorized as a medical strategy (see Chapter Nineteen).

However, this strategy has a special strength. Many of the people who will be helped have been carrying the burden of a debilitated family member for years. They are exhausted and desperate for help. Prior to the arrival of your team, most likely they have had no one to whom they could turn. From the moment that you enter into their lives, you bring love, compassion, and optimism. Unlike any other strategy, you continually are bringing therapeutic physical touch to those in great need. The impact is commonly profound. I can think of nothing that more endears one to a family in such a short amount of time, thus assuring the greatest potential for receptivity when making disciples.

As in the hospice strategy, the specialist making the evaluation does not necessarily do the majority of the therapy. Instead, the specialist makes an evaluative visit with a member of the rehab team, a member whom he trains to perform the needed tasks. These nonprofessional *rehab technicians* will continue to meet with the patient as directed by the rehab specialist, usually a few times per week. During that time, the technician will also train family members to perform the needed therapy so that the patient is being helped every day. Periodically, the rehab specialist must return to the home to check on the patient's progress and to train the technician in any new skills that may be needed.

In just a short amount of time, the rehab technician becomes special to the family. From the beginning he or she can pray for the patient and can unfold the Gospel in ways best for that culture.

IMPLICATIONS FOR A
CHURCH-PLANTING MOVEMENT

Imagine that you are a hard-hearted religious fundamentalist, completely closed to outside ideas. Now imagine that God has given you a child with a birth defect. You have been told stories of similar tragedies and have believed these disabilities were punishment from God for a past sin. As you search your heart, you do not believe that to be the case, but you cannot explain why this has happened. For this reason, you decide to get your child the best of care but try to hide the problem.

Doctors tell you that there is no treatment and do not offer anything besides some token pills. You do your best to feed, bathe, and love your child as the years go by. Over time, the child gets heavier and more difficult to handle. Your neighbors all know that you have a disabled child, but they are polite enough to never mention the subject. Your family carries the burden alone.

Can you see how readily you would welcome even an outsider who had come to help with your child? Although you may have been closed to the idea, your previous beliefs have failed you, and you are eager to be taught anything helpful.

If your rehabilitation team can work with dozens of families such as this, they can easily present the Gospel, and as the Holy Spirit draws them, disciples will be made. This new church can use their experience to preach and heal through several small rehab teams, hospice teams, or Luke 10 teams.

CHAPTER 13

COMMUNITY DEVELOPMENT

Enter the Community	Make Disciples	Empower the Church
✪ ✪ ✪	✪ ✪ ✪	✪ ✪ ✪

✔ URBAN ✔ RURAL ◯ DEVELOPED ✔ DEVELOPING

- Almost half of the world's inhabitants live on less than two dollars per day.
- One-third of the world's population lacks access to essential medicines.
- 2.4 billion people, 38 percent of humanity, lack access to proper sanitation.
- Up to 75 percent of women in some populations report being regularly beaten at home.[10]

Our truck slid along the muddy grooves of the only road into the village. It was one of the poorer communities in the area. Houses were small and in disrepair with hanging burlap rather than glass in the windows. Loose dogs and thin, ragged children ran to our vehicle. Adults were sitting outside on a work day and did not rise to greet us. No one seemed to be doing anything productive.

We sat outside with the village leaders, our feet in mud as we drank their smoky tea and listened to them complain about life. They told stories of women dying in childbirth, children dying during the winter, a contaminated water supply, no sanitation, no schools, and crops that wouldn't grow. It was as if we had been transported to a village of cavemen. Life was about survival, and they were doing it poorly.

THE PROBLEM

I could tell more stories and show you more statistics that would, or at least should, break your heart. Most of the world is hurting. People live in poverty, illiteracy, illness, and violence. They are subjected to wars, harsh living conditions, culturally abhorrent practices (such as female genital mutilation), and caste systems that ensure individual and community stagnation. They are forced into perpetuating child labor, debt bondage, human trafficking, and gender inequality. Worst of all, they are prisoners of ignorance effectively partitioned from the knowledge of God's glorious gift to humankind and thereby encapsulated in hopelessness and fear.

Remember the problem of compartmentalization. Because we are from a highly specialized culture, we tend to compartmentalize problems and focus on those areas with which we are most comfortable. A water engineer may attempt to bring clean water to a community, a teacher may want to improve education, and a nurse may try to decrease the incidence of disease.

A holistic approach, however, looks at the whole person and the whole community. It seeks to address physical, emotional, social, moral, economic, and perhaps spiritual issues under the banner of *community development* (CD).

Community development workers are everywhere in the developing world. The majority are secular and care about improving the physical lives of target communities. They use terms like "needs assessment," "capacity building," and "sustainability."

These workers and their organizations usually survive from grants to help the needy people of the world. They develop thorough plans for improving living conditions, they receive money for these plans, and they work their agenda until the funding runs out or they meet their objectives.

There are also many "Christian" community development organizations and workers. There is little difference in the modus operandi of Christian and secular organizations. Both are competent and effective at helping the needy. Christian organizations ordinarily state that they do their work in the name of Jesus. The objective of almost all of these agencies is to see human lives improve, but it is not to see an indigenous multiplying church sweeping through the land. Christian CD workers are virtually all healers. People do come to Christ by their witness, but the growth of the church is modestly additive rather than multiplicative. They are not ordinarily in the business of empowering national disciples to reach their nation with the Gospel.

THE STRATEGY

Church planters have much to learn from the community development school. CD workers are in communities meeting the needs of hurting people and training nationals. In many cases, CD workers have effectively entered the community, are visiting in homes, and are well-positioned to make disciples. Unfortunately, they generally fall short in disciple-making. Because making multiplying disciples is not their measure of success, they do not intentionally pursue this agenda.

A good community development strategy should exhibit those practices that are consistent with good CD, but will be fashioned in such a way that enables workers to make disciples and empower the church. The result will be families and communities that have not only been improved physically, emotionally, and socially but who have been transformed through a right relationship with the Creator.

CORE VALUES

Just like any discipline, community development has evolved over the years. In the past, emphasis was placed on giving hurting people what they wanted. Today emphasis is placed on developing the people being served. There are also many other principles that would be considered as foundational for appropriate CD work. From these I have chosen only those that are also conducive to establishing multiplying indigenous churches to form a list of "core values" for the community development strategy.

1. True health is whole health: If you can remember the first two parts of this book, then you understand that true health is whole health. People are more than just physical *or* spiritual beings. Jesus commanded us to address the needs of both human components.

Secular community development addresses issues such as preventable diseases, agriculture, nutrition, drug abuse, and domestic violence. The community development strategy, however, also addresses the issue that produces these symptoms. All work is built upon the premise that the world is under a curse and the influence of Satan. God has offered a sacrifice through His Son, and His blood has the power to break the curse from any individual. One may still live in a cursed world, but he can have freedom from the curse for his family. Freedom from the curse is the first step in overcoming social, emotional, and even physical woes. The community development strategy asserts that this message must be taught within the heart of the community by every practitioner.

2. Home visits: A short visit into many homes in the developing world will reveal the reason for problems that families experience. You will find chickens and their droppings in the house, babies sucking on filthy toys, mothers washing dishes without hot water or soap, people sitting down to a meal with dirty hands and clothes, all family members drinking unsafe water, and food prepared with no thought to proper nutrition. You don't even want to see the bathroom. For this reason, visiting in homes is essential for good community development and recognizing the needs of a given community. I would also add that teaching about disease prevention, nutrition, or other health issues is more effective in homes than out in the open.

At the same time, effective Gospel communication and disciple making can only take place in an environment where there will be no interruptions and in which one's audience is comfortable. The best place for this is often "behind closed doors" inside homes. Being inside homes provides the opportunity to teach the entire family, important both for good CD and for disciple making.

3. Nationals training nationals: Because community development is mostly about training (requiring best communication), CD organizations use trained nationals to teach. This practice is also most conducive to effective evangelizing, disciple making, and empowering the church. Foreign workers should be language competent and work in homes. But it is best to have foreigners working alongside national disciples. In this way, the foreigners can model daily communication of the Gospel, methods of evangelism, and a passion for the lost. The foreign workers should always defer the primary task of teaching to these national disciples and quickly should hand off the tasks of community development training and disciple making.

At this point let me make a provocative suggestion. Normal operating procedure for CD organizations, whether secular or Christian, is to hire nationals as salaried workers. When someone works for you with regularity and for many hours, it seems right to compensate them. Yet, the rules for things related to God's kingdom often don't follow normal operating procedures. The most costly mistakes are made when we treat the business of heaven the same way we do the business of earth. Disciples work from an eternal perspective with a heavenly culture and follow principles that are ordinarily at odds with logic.

At one time, I was part of a team operating medical and community development projects in rural areas. None of us spoke the local language, and we needed national translators. Almost immediately, we met a few men who had become disciples of Jesus from a Muslim background. They asked us to teach them more about Christ. We asked them to be volunteer translators in exchange. After two months, we had about 10 of these disciples working several days each week, often for 10-hour days in the snow without getting any salary.

On days when not enough of these men were available, we *hired* Muslim translators. Before doing this, we explained the situation to the disciples. "For now," we told them, "we are providing services for the poor people in remote villages. But we will not be here forever and when we leave, you will be going alone to care for the poor. When you help them and tell them about Jesus, the villagers will certainly ask you how much you are being paid, expecting that you have converted because of a financial benefit. At that time, we want you to be able to say that you have never received money from the Americans and do this work because of your love for the poor and your obedience to Jesus."

At this the men all said, "That is excellent. Never give me a salary so that I do not ruin the quality of my witness." Later, when the disciples would work alongside Muslim workers who were being paid, they would brag about how they were not taking a salary and were serving the poor out of charity. This became a way in which they were able to witness to these Muslim friends.

There may be situations in which you must place national disciples/community development workers in a remote town or need someone for 40 hours each week. In that case, it may be necessary to give a salary. It is always best, if possible, for even that money to come from among the national disciples themselves. Remember the resources are in the harvest. Even if there are only 10 disciples in a city, their offerings can support a full-time worker doing charity work. It may be a great strain on them, but it will ultimately be a great benefit to that church and will set a standard for future work.

4. Oral-based training: Oral-based communication seeks to give information through oral stories or plays. As an example, a lesson about intestinal parasites may be a story with the following points:

1. A child plays in the dirt with her hands.
2. She eats bread without washing her hands.
3. The child gets symptoms of abdominal pain, fever, and headache.
4. The family tries traditional healings, but the child does not improve.
5. A health worker visits the family and explains the connection between soiled hands and getting intestinal worms.
6. The child is taken to the doctor, given a medicine, and improves.
7. The family institutes a rule of washing hands before meals.
8. The child doesn't get worms ever again.

To solidify the lesson in the minds of the audience, the national disciples/community development workers should tell the story to one another several times and be instructed to tell it in the community numerous times that week. In the same way, instruction about Jesus should be given through stories. When presenting the Gospel, I tell Bible stories that make the following points:

1. Where Satan and sin came from
2. How the world became cursed by sin
3. God's promise, through the prophets, to send someone to remove the curse
4. How God sent Jesus and how He proved Himself to be from God
5. How Jesus overcame the curse
6. The promise of a heaven where there is no more curse
7. What every person must do now to be saved from the curse

I use this format not only among people who can't read but also among the highly educated. Among all of the cultures where I work, the majority of people are still oral learners. Practitioners should learn to teach an oral-based Gospel in just one hour and how to present it in multiple visits. (I have included a short version as Appendix E and placed a long version on the Internet at http://mmronline.org/resources.aspx.)

5. Community ownership: One of the greatest mistakes of some past work in community development and in church planting was that of paternalism. In some cases, our arrogance led us to assume a position in which we placed ourselves as the perpetual fathers and leaders of all work, whether secular or spiritual. Even when we were not acting out of arrogance, we often allowed nationals to manipulate us into taking that position of leadership so that we would provide more for them.

When paternalism was prevalent, development of the community was greatly retarded, and any progress had disappeared within years of the departure of expatriate leaders. In the same way, churches started were crippled when the foreign apostolic workers moved on, rarely becoming healthy or multiplying.

From the very beginning, nationals must participate in decision making so that they can catch the vision, both for developing their community and for spiritual transformation of the whole nation. They must internalize ownership and take the positions of leadership.

When troubles arise, the indigenous leadership should solve the problem in the community development program and in the church. In that way, the church learns to pray together and depend upon the Holy Spirit to supply all of their needs rather than deferring to foreigners and foreign resources.

6. Development rather than relief: In general, *relief* can be thought of as providing for those in need. An example would be giving blankets to homeless people after an earthquake. *Development* can be thought of as community growth. An example would be teaching mothers how to provide safe water for their families. Relief work is usually more about giving whereas development work is more about training and empowering.

Providing relief is biblical, and I will discuss ideas about a relief strategy later in this section. But we are now focused on community development, and this calls for a different mindset and approach. Development seeks to improve the community through developing the people. The answers and resources to most problems are right there in the community. Again, I remind you of the dictum: the resources are in the harvest.

Since the resources for improvement are present already or obtainable, it is difficult to know why some communities solve their own problems while others remain stagnant. Solutions typically fail to be implemented because of lack of initiative, lack of cooperation, an entitlement mindset, or many other factors that may very well be related to the community's spiritual condition.

I hypothesize the primary problem as spiritual because of a phenomenon that is commonly seen. In those communities where a healthy church is established, development of the community is more often successful and lasting. But communities seem more likely to be stuck in the quagmire of underdevelopment when only secular community development is attempted. This has caused some apostolic workers to argue that the best path to community improvement is through church planting without any care for the needy. However, we aren't going down that path because our objective is not to find a way that seems best to us but to do our best to be obedient to the teachings of our Lord Christ. We will help those in need and establish a multiplying church.

7. Spontaneous multiplication: One of the strengths of community development is that it provides much secure interaction with nationals. Your apostolic team is constantly in the community, and you soon gain a reputation for being servants of the community. Because of this reputation and the fact that your CD work always puts you in a position of training, you can easily come and go from many homes. This is essential for making disciples and for empowering the church.

It is hoped that everything learned by the community will be passed on to other communities so that the community development strategy will perpetuate. My experience, though, shows that it usually doesn't happen in the planned way. There are many examples of the recipients of CD taking their knowledge to other communities, but it is more common for the new disciples to begin taking very effective shortcuts.

Disciples made through the community development strategy frequently approach foreign workers with a plan to move to an unreached community or state. They plan to use much of what they have learned, but they don't generally plan to start a full CD program; after all, they usually don't have a large team or a vehicle. Instead, they will break off with a partner, enter an unreached area, and utilize something like a simple Luke 10 strategy with some family teaching about health. Or they may set up a little office as a base from which they go to visit poor widows, the chronically ill, or malnourished children.

The core values of community development

1. True health is whole health
2. Home visits
3. Nationals training nationals
4. Oral-based training
5. Community ownership
6. Development rather than relief
7. Spontaneous multiplication

These core values are the overlap between good community development and good church-planting strategy. As you can see, the principles needed to develop a community are the same as those needed to develop disciples and provide a place for you to empower those disciples on to a disciple-making movement. For this reason, one can be completely open about these values and can share them with the authorities before beginning any work. Write up a document to explain why you are entering homes, training nationals, and even teaching spiritual lessons alongside lessons on physical, emotional, and social health.

IMPLICATIONS FOR
A CHURCH-PLANTING MOVEMENT

I recently moved my family into a completely Muslim area to help initiate a community development strategy. The target area was at war, so we were based in a city just a short distance away. In addition to my family, two nurses and another doctor had come as volunteers. Our medical/ community development team would travel by helicopter into the remote target area, camp for one to two weeks, and would then return to the city for a few days to rest and get new supplies.

Since there were no medical services in the entire area, we began our project by providing free medical care. We only did this for the first three weeks, seeing as many patients as we could each day, demonstrating the love from Christ as best as we could, and giving medicines and our time generously.

We had met a true man of peace on our first day, and after we had finished our three weeks of medical services, we told him of our desire to implement a program that would prevent the majority of the diseases that we had been seeing. He heartily agreed with this idea and arranged for us to meet with their community leadership on the next day.

There were nine Muslim men at this meeting who warmly conveyed their thanks for the work that we had been doing to help them in their time of crisis. We told them that we had concluded our free medical clinic and also told them about the diseases that we had found to be very common in their community, explaining that most of these diseases were preventable. We then asked the question, "Is there anything else you would like us to do for you?" and sat quietly.

The men talked among themselves for about two minutes and then said, "Yes. Can you please stay here and teach us how to prevent these diseases? We will bring 30 volunteers together each week, you can teach health lessons to them, and they will take the lessons back to every village in the area." I am not embellishing this story. Within 15 minutes, this group of community leaders had proposed a structure that was perfect for us to help thousands of hurting families and to present the Gospel to many different audiences.

Two days later, 35 men gathered in a community building, and our small team began to teach them the basics of community development. We gave each man a notebook and pen and congratulated them on their willingness to become volunteer community health workers. We began with three skits that demonstrated the seven core values of good CD and had the learners repeat each skit at least two more times. After about two hours, we broke for lunch.

In the afternoon session we told a story about intestinal worms, and I told the story about the origin of sin in heaven and how Satan brought it to earth. I explained about the earth being placed under a curse and about God's promise to send someone who would break the curse and restore our relationship with Him. I only spoke for about 30 minutes.

The next week, we had 40 men at the training. We asked for feedback about the prior week's training and got nothing but praise. In the morning session, we taught about safe water, dehydration, and how to make oral rehydration solution using clean water, salt, sugar, and local lime. We had learned the formula and the information from the book Where There Is No Doctor.

In the afternoon session, we taught lessons about dysentery and spiritual health. I explained how God instituted the practice of blood sacrifice through Moses but then sent many prophets who taught that God would fulfill His promise to send a curse-breaker, the ultimate blood sacrifice for the sins of the people. Then I told the story about Jesus' miraculous birth.

On the next week, we had almost 50 men and a few boys come to the training. We asked for feedback about the training since I was concerned that there may be objections to the teaching about Jesus. On the contrary, they maintained that they loved the training. No one else had ever spent time with them, teaching them how they could live healthier lives. They promised that they were gathering the people in their villages and were repeating the lessons.

We were scheduled to leave the area in just a few days. At our last training session before a permanent team took over, we ambitiously taught about malaria, schistosomiasis (a disease that we had found to be common in the area), and nutrition. In the afternoon we were running late, so the translator said, "Dr. Charles, please let these men go for prayers." I was disappointed as I still had not shared the final stories about Jesus, but I didn't want to force the Gospel on them. Someone had donated 50 bags of gardening seeds to the project, so we gave them each a bag of seeds before they left. For those who were interested, I would stay to tell the last story about Jesus.

Each of the men came to the front by the door and collected a bag, but returned to their seats. All of them wanted to hear the story rather than go to Muslim prayers. So I told them how Jesus demonstrated Himself to be God's Son by performing many miracles. I then detailed the facts about the crucifixion, resurrection, His ascension, the Day of Pentecost, and how Jesus will return again to judge the world.

At the conclusion of the story, I apologized that I had kept the men so long, and a middle-aged man in the group interrupted me. "Dr. Charles," he said. "Please do not apologize. There is nothing more important than the things that you have been teaching us today."

After this we stood at the door and shook hands with each man as he left, inviting them all to return that night for a party. After they had gone and as I was washing my hands, I had a thought that I know was from the Lord. Prior to coming to the area, I had prayed constantly that I would be able to share the Gospel at least once each day we were in this remote area. I had presented the Gospel to our man of peace/translator on several occasions but since he was the only English speaker in the area, I was disappointed that I had not been able to share the Gospel on other days. The message from the Lord was very sweet. He said, "Charles, do you remember your prayers prior to coming here? You have only spent 40 nights in this place, and you feel as if you have missed 40 opportunities to share the Gospel, but I have just given you a way to present the Gospel to 50 people." By the way, over 200 people came to our party that night, and we had a wonderful time together.

Just like the Luke 10 strategy, the community development strategy is a hallmark for health strategies. Even if you choose another strategy, the principles of good CD should be utilized so that you do not fall into one of the many traps that have caught apostolic workers in the past.

We have seen the community development strategy utilized in some of the most restricted areas of the world; it effectively gets behind closed doors, and it cares for the needy. Therefore, this strategy readily follows the ABCs. You will also find that the next two strategies, "family wellness" and "slums, refugee camps, and prisons," are closely related, following the same CD principles. These strategies keep in mind the reasons why unreached peoples are unreached and overcome those barriers. Yet, these are not silver bullets. We have seen teams use the CD strategy to bring about a church-planting movement among their people group, and we have seen a team utilize the strategy, seemingly doing everything right for years, with very few results. For this reason, we enter into this work with much prayer, depending upon the guidance of the Lord, and looking to Him to bring about a Christward movement through His power.

CHAPTER 14

FAMILY WELLNESS

Enter the Community	Make Disciples	Empower the Church
✪ ✪ ✪	✪ ✪ ✪	✪ ✪ ✪

☑ URBAN ☑ RURAL ◯ DEVELOPED ☑ DEVELOPING

Perhaps everywhere in the world, the mother of the house is the primary health provider for the family. In English we call her "Doctor Mom." In addition to taking care of us when we are sick, the ladies of the house constantly keep us well by keeping the house, our clothes, and the dishes clean; by making sure that family members bathe and wash their hands before meals; by making sure the children learn how to brush their teeth; and by buying and serving healthy foods.

Dads aren't always as contributory in this arena, but they do have some part to play. Although certainly not as indispensable as Doctor Mom, fathers are ordinarily responsible for maintaining and warming the family shelter, perhaps for maintaining a garden, and for other home improvements that have health implications.

THE PROBLEM

In developing countries, women frequently have much less education. Because of that, their family wellness practices may be in great
need of improvement. Issues that are common sense to most of us
are not at all common in these homes. Families continue to stay sick,
spending money on medicines and missing days of work, because
they drink unsafe water and milk, live in unhealthy environments,
or have infections from poor hygiene and nutrition.

In these same places, illiteracy rates among women are high,
so teaching documents or lectures are not likely to be beneficial.
In general, these women have learned their current housekeeping
practices from their mothers, and they can best learn an alternative
practice by having someone else show them a new approach. As for
dads, they may have had no information about home improvements
that could prevent diseases.

THE STRATEGY

Well, you can see where this is going. These families need someone
to come into their houses every week or so, to teach them the basics
of family wellness. Most of the teaching is done by showing them
common family health practices, but teaching also can be done by
telling made-up stories about diseases and explaining how to prevent
those diseases.

With this understanding, one structures a family wellness
strategy the same as a community development strategy. You enter
the community, make disciples, and empower the church the same
way, but teaching focuses on those subjects that will help a family
to be healthy.

This strategy doesn't have to be completely about women. In
addressing nutrition, a team could teach men how to compost and
prepare a garden that will provide nutritious food for the family. They
could also teach men how to improve the family's sanitation facili-
ties and how to make water safe for drinking. If appropriate, they
could teach them how to put screens in the windows and mosquito

netting over beds to prevent malaria or other diseases. The point is that the team is working toward family development rather than community development.

FAMILY HEALTH CLUBS

If you would like to do it with flair, you could even establish family health clubs in these target communities. These clubs could supplement the house-to-house training by having monthly gatherings of families to discuss the progress of the program, to decide what issues need to be addressed, or to hear a guest teacher. Go crazy if you want to and have a logo, a slogan, printed T-shirts, baseball caps, and an annual party—anything to increase enthusiasm for the overall program so that the house-to-house visits will be welcomed.

In one area, a team wanted to have a family health strategy, but the communities were too big to visit every home. Their person of peace in two communities was the principal at the school, so they decided to restrict the program to families that had school-age children. The persons of peace were also concerned about the health issues in the communities; therefore, the team arranged to have a volunteer doctor perform health screenings on the children. The doctor identified a few health issues that were prevalent among the children. This information was taken back to the persons of peace.

The team explained that they would like to teach health classes to the school children but thought that it would be best to do this after school. Health, they explained, is a family issue, and it is best to teach these lessons with the whole family present. So they proposed choosing volunteers from the community who their team would train on health issues each week. These volunteers would then take the lessons into each home that had school-age children. They called the program "The Family Health Club." The persons of peace, who were already authorities over education, readily accepted this plan. The lessons began at the start of the school year.

This team had lived among their people group for five years but had almost no success in making disciples. Within a few months, though, there were new churches in both communities. They also reported that the strategy brought their team together in an unprecedented way as they each worked together for a common purpose.

MATERNAL/CHILD WELLNESS

A variation on this model would be to only work in families with a pregnant woman or where a child has just been born. The teaching would be focused more on how to have a healthy pregnancy and how to keep the newborn child well for the first two years of life.

Issues could be:

- How to eat nutritional foods and take prenatal vitamins during pregnancy
- How to prepare for delivery
- How to care for a newborn
- How to get immunizations for a baby

One benefit to this approach is that it could be done in larger communities where a classic family wellness strategy, which goes into every home, would be impossible. Also, it has a pre-set time parameter of about two years, giving plenty of time for an incarnational team to work through all of the components of intentional church planting and then leaving behind national disciples who have been trained in maternal/child wellness and multiplicative church planting.

PICK A TOPIC

As you have seen, a community development strategy is great for positioning your team for success, but it isn't always easy to pull off. If your team is small or your target area is largely populated, it would be difficult to implement. A team can help overcome this problem by narrowing the percentage of people who would receive services. The family health club and maternal/child wellness strategy are examples, but another approach would be to focus on only one disease and its prevention. The examples of tuberculosis, malnutrition, and AIDS warrant their own chapters and will be covered later, but it would be very reasonable to address one problem such as intestinal parasites, tooth decay, diarrhea, eye problems, lice, or any other problem that is relevant to your target group.

With very little study, you can become an expert in your chosen field and can move from community to community treating, preventing, and teaching. In one area, we began a program called "Waging War on Worms." In each school, we instructed about intestinal parasites and distributed worm pills, gaining credibility in the region. We soon adapted our strategy so that we were moving in and out of homes.

IMPLICATIONS FOR A
CHURCH-PLANTING MOVEMENT

This strategy can't be used just anywhere. It is mainly for developing countries in which people have had a limited education. But in those instances, any strategies that work with families are likely to be greatly appreciated by that audience. Entering the community should be a snap. Again, we have seen this strategy used to access completely restricted areas, to mobilize disciple makers behind closed doors, and to care for the needy.

And here is something to keep in mind about teaching women. In some cultures, in addition to being the matrons over health, women are also the keepers of religion. It is frequently the women who insist that the family says their prayers or sets aside money for religious education for the children. It is also common for uneducated women in many of these cultures to have a fascination with the supernatural. If effective disciple making and the accompanying supernatural experience of meeting and knowing Jesus were to hit these women, the potential is there for the Gospel to spread throughout a people group.

CHAPTER 15

SLUMS, REFUGEE CAMPS, AND PRISONS

Enter the Community	Make Disciples	Empower the Church
✪ ✪ ✪	✪ ✪ ✪	✪ ✪ ✪

✓URBAN ✓RURAL ◯DEVELOPED ✓DEVELOPING

If anyone has this world's goods and sees his brother in need but shuts off his compassion from him—how can God's love reside in him? (I John 3:17)

If a brother or sister is without clothes and lacks daily food, and one of you says to them, "Go in peace, keep warm, and eat well," but you don't give them what the body needs, what good is it? In the same way faith, if it doesn't have works, is dead by itself (James 2:15-17).

"When did we see You sick, or in prison, and visit You?" And the King will answer them, "I assure you: Whatever you did for one of the least of these brothers of Mine, you did for Me" (Matthew 25:39-40).

THE PROBLEM

The world is changing. It is becoming crowded, and there is an unprecedented scramble for her resources. In the year 2007, for the first time in history, more people lived in cities than in rural areas. The cities of the world have nowhere to put all of these people, much less give them all jobs. For this reason, a large proportion of those going to the city for a better life will end up in slums.

At present, about 100 million people live in a slum.[11] The number of slum inhabitants is expected to double over the next 25 years. In the least-developed countries, the situation is much worse with up to 78 percent of the urban population living in slums. You may find this hard to believe because these cities do not look that bad off while driving the streets. However, although the number of slum inhabitants may be as high as three in four, the amount of city land that they occupy is often a percentage in single digits.

The situation in these slums is getting worse. The total number of slum inhabitants in the world increased by about 36 percent during the 1990s. During that same decade, the number of slum inhabitants without access to adequate water increased by 290 percent. I am sorry to turn your stomach, but 40 percent of slum inhabitants do not have access to proper sanitation and literally live amid their own waste.[12]

The lack of world resources, among other things, has resulted in many conflicts with huge populations being displaced from their homes in search of peace and a livelihood. These 37 million people are scattered around the globe commonly settled in refugee or internally displaced people (IDP) camps.[13] IDPs have been forced from their homes but still reside within their own country. Refugees also have been forced from their homes but have crossed an international border in their flight.

Another consequence of rapid urbanization has been an increase in crime. As you can imagine, this has resulted in overcrowded and under-resourced prisons. Again, in developing nations, this problem is significantly compounded, making prisons among the unhealthiest places in those societies.[14]

THE STRATEGY

There is no one strategy for impacting slums, refugee camps, or prisons. If you have been paying attention, though, you should be able to take the principles that you have learned and construct a variety of strategies for these situations. To make it easier, I'll walk through it with you.

The first step is to determine how you will enter the community following the ABCs. As you think through these steps, keep the later objectives of *make disciples* and *empower the church* in mind so that you will not head down a strategic cul-de-sac.

As for the "A," it is up to you to honestly admit whether or not you are accessing *unreached* areas. The question to be asked is: Will some people in this community (not all or many) hear the Gospel in their lifetime? Look around. Are there churches or other evangelical ministries present? If the answer is yes, move on to an area or region where people do not have access to the Gospel.

The "B" of *getting behind closed doors* is the first strategic challenge, but think of how much easier this can be in settings such as slums and refugee camps. These areas are commonly ignored by the larger society and are desperate for help. In my experience, they are among the easiest communities to access. In fact, I have been invited into more of these homes and tents than I can remember. And I have always found an open audience.

One could easily utilize a Luke 10, community development, or family health strategy to access these communities. One of our dear friends was a Korean/American nurse working in South Asia. Her house was near a slum area and after making a friend there, she began visiting. She led this friend to Jesus and asked her to invite some women to hear a talk about healthier housekeeping. Thirty women came on the first visit, and she taught them how to use soap and warm water to wash dishes. After a few more classes, she had over 60 women, virtually every woman in the little community, coming to her training sessions. She brought women forward to demonstrate many things such as how to wash one's hair with shampoo and how to brush one's teeth. As she visited in their homes, she led several of those women to the Lord. I still don't know how she did it since she had moved to the region after the age of 60 and didn't speak any of the local language.

There are no solid doors in prison, so you must decide whether or not your host culture would allow you to share the Gospel in a cell setting. We have been surprised to find that some closed cultures have allowed the Gospel to be shared, the *JESUS*film to be shown, and the Bible to be distributed within their prisons. Of course, this was done after performing significant services for the prisoners, such as treating them for scabies and tuberculosis or helping with vocational training.

This brings us to the "C" of *care for the needy*. The needs of slum inhabitants, refugees, and prisoners are more than any other members of a community. I have frequently made the mistake of asking the question, "What do you need?" The reply is, "We need everything." When deciding how to care for the needy, keep in mind the next step of *make disciples* and go after those needs that will best lead you to that end. Once disciples are made, *empower the church* by teaching them how to make disciples among their neighbors and how to gather into indigenous churches that will multiply throughout the community.

IMPLICATIONS FOR A CHURCH-PLANTING MOVEMENT

If only the humble can enter the kingdom of heaven, then slums, refugee camps, and prisons are the places to go looking for them. Indeed, the great majority of church-planting movements have been among the poor and people in turmoil. Actually, this trend goes all the way back to the beginning, as indicated in James 2:5: "Listen, my dear brothers: Didn't God choose the poor in this world to be rich in faith and heirs of the kingdom that He has promised to those who love Him?"

CHAPTER 16

TUBERCULOSIS DOTS

Enter the Community	Make Disciples	Empower the Church
✪ ✪ ✪	✪ ✪ ✪	✪ ✪

✔URBAN   ✔RURAL   ◯DEVELOPED   ✔DEVELOPING

- One-third of all people have tuberculosis (TB).
- There are 9 million new cases of TB each year.
- Ninety-eight percent of TB deaths occur in the developing world.
- A person with active TB infects 10 to 15 people per year.[15]

No one knows how long tuberculosis has been around. It has been reported in ancient literature, and has even been found in 4,000-year-old Egyptian mummies. Hippocrates, the father of medicine, reported it as the most prevalent of all diseases in 460 B.C. He recommended that physicians avoid visiting patients in later stages of the disease because the patient's certain death would hurt the physician's reputation.

Tuberculosis is primarily a disease of the lungs. Patients with this form of the disease have a chronic cough, which sometimes contains blood. Patients also lose weight and energy so that the disease was known for centuries as "consumption."

Although one-third of all people are infected with tuberculosis, the majority of these people carry a "latent" infection—that is, the bacteria has been effectively walled off by the immune system and is not causing any active disease. Of course, if a person's immune system is compromised by AIDS, malnutrition, or other factors, the TB can become active and can even lead to death. About 10 percent of latent infections will become active.

THE PROBLEM

When the AIDS epidemic came along, many latent infections "woke up" in AIDS patients so that the incidence of active TB has risen dramatically over the past 15 years. As a result, the World Health Organization declared in 1993 that tuberculosis was a global health emergency.

The proper treatment for TB is for a patient to take several different medicines (causing side effects) every day for over six months. Many TB patients found this cost-prohibitive, or otherwise unacceptable, and took medicine until they felt better. They discontinued the medicine when they seemed well.

The problem, however, was that they were not completely well. While in treatment, the medicines killed the most susceptible bacteria but when they quit the medicines, the toughest germs were still alive and began to multiply. After awhile, the TB cough of these persons returned, and they began coughing out germs that infected other people. These toughest germs were resistant to the usual medicines.

Some of these new germs can be killed if a patient takes even more medicines for an even longer period of time, and some of them can't be killed by any of the current medicines. The result—a massive increase in tuberculosis, a disease we considered to be a problem of the past, with some of these cases now highly resistant to existing treatments.

THE STRATEGY

Because of the enormity of this problem, many health organizations came together to develop a strategy to fight TB. There were a variety of strategies and disagreements for years, but one strategy has now been accepted as the most effective and has been adopted by everyone as the international standard. It is called Direct Observation Therapy Short-course (DOTS).

DOTS works like this. Once a person is diagnosed with tuberculosis, his name and contact information is registered at a TB control center, and a plan is made to assure that the patient gets all medicines for the full treatment course. A member of a DOTS team actually gives the medicine every day and watches the patient swallow the pills. After a few months, the patient only needs medicines a few times each week until the treatment is complete. The specifics of treatment vary from place to place, but the cornerstone of the strategy is that the DOTS worker directly observes the patient taking the medicine throughout the entire treatment course. If the patient lives near the TB control center, he can come in for the meds. If he lives in a remote community, another plan is needed. The DOTS team can visit the patient daily, or someone in the community can be trained as a volunteer DOTS worker.

By working with community leaders, a volunteer is selected for training. Often the person chosen already has healthcare responsibilities in the community. The training for the DOTS volunteer covers two areas: treating the current patient and finding new cases of TB. Treatment consists of making sure the patient takes medicine as directed by the physician but also covers improving nutritional intake, which is particularly important for the treatment of tuberculosis.

The beauty of this strategy is that it is a universally accepted program, developed by the World Health Organization (WHO) and other international aid entities. There is much literature to tell you exactly how to follow through with the program, there are UN and WHO offices to help with problems, and there may be international aid money available. Additionally, a DOTS program is very simple and does not require a healthcare background for anyone working in the program.

IMPLICATIONS FOR A
CHURCH-PLANTING MOVEMENT

We decided to try a TB DOTS strategy among a completely unreached mountain people group in a very poor country. The apostolic minister who championed the project was 65 years old and had no healthcare background. He and his wife were supposed to have retired until they heard about this people group of 1 million Muslims who had no known disciples and no Gospel witness.

Our first step was to see how the health authorities felt about the idea, so we visited the minister of health for the region. He was rather unimpressed by our visit until we mentioned the word "tuberculosis." He said, "Tuberculosis is my biggest problem here. I will do anything to help you if you will address that issue."

The next meeting was with the World Health Organization representative who promised to give free training to any worker and free medicines to every patient. He also said that he would obtain a monthly gift of free food from the World Food Program for every tuberculosis patient treated.

Our objective was to treat 200 tuberculosis patients and to advance the Gospel into many remote communities within two years. At that time, the only workers were this "almost retired" couple.

Possibly because the strategy was attractive, but probably because the apostolic workers were giants in prayer, many young and talented workers quickly joined the team. At the two-year mark, there were six apostolic families working on the project. They had met the goal of treating 200 patients, sustained access into over 60 villages never visited by apostolic ministers of Jesus, and trained over 100 TB volunteers whom they continued to visit frequently. This team had quickly moved through the "enter the community" stage of church-planting strategy and was in the process of making disciples while other teams in the country were not able to get into restricted villages or into national homes.

Tuberculosis is a terrible and frightening disease. Those with TB slowly waste away, and family members are torn between the desire to help the sick and the fear of catching the disease themselves. Because of the manpower hours required, governments are rarely capable of providing the appropriate treatment, that is DOTS, to every community. What a wonderful opportunity for followers of Jesus Christ to enter these communities and not only attack this physical killer but darkness as well.

CHAPTER 17

MALNUTRITION

Enter the Community	Make Disciples	Empower the Church
★ ★ ★	★ ★ ★	★ ★ ★

✔ URBAN ✔ RURAL ◯ DEVELOPED ✔ DEVELOPING

- One-half of deaths in children under the age of five are related to malnutrition.
- Eighty percent of malnutrition related deaths are among children who are only mildly or moderately malnourished.[16]
- One in 10 young children in developing countries is undernourished.
- Malnutrition remains the greatest cause of health loss in the world.[17]

"Too many children die each year, mostly during the wintertime," the elder complained. *"They get many sicknesses, like diarrhea or the flu, and they just stay sick until they die."*

But the children didn't look that bad off. They were thin with runny noses and a few skin infections but overall, they appeared fairly healthy.

"What do they eat?" the doctor asked.

"We eat rice with every meal, and we add some vegetables on top. Of course, when the snow comes, we do not have the vegetables."

"How long does the snow last?" asked the doctor.

"Oh, it begins in October and sometimes stays until May."

"So the children just eat rice during that time?"

"Yes, mostly just rice and some bread."

THE PROBLEM

In the developing world, most preventable deaths are among children less than five years old, a well-known fact for health authorities in developing countries. These authorities concentrate on programs designed to improve the health of the young.

When one looks at the statistics, it seems clear that diarrhea is the main killer of children followed by malaria, pneumonia, and other infectious diseases. Western children get diarrhea, but they don't die. They also get common colds that almost never progress to pneumonia. So what is the difference?

The difference is nutrition. Undernourished children are not only deficient in daily caloric intake, but they are also undernourished in minerals, vitamins, and proteins. Children don't commonly die from poor nutrition, but it is the world's leading risk factor for death by other infectious causes. You can think of it in the same way that you think of smoking. Smoking doesn't kill people, but a smoker is nine times more likely to die of lung cancer than a nonsmoker. In the same way, poor nutrition usually doesn't kill children, but a poorly nourished child has a greatly increased chance of succumbing to otherwise non-threatening infections.

The reason is simple. An undernourished child has decreased immunity. The body has internal agents that fight a battle against germs. The response to these invaders comes in different forms, and there are many factors and mediators making sure that the response is timely and effective. Protein and calories can be thought of like gasoline, and vitamins and minerals can be thought of as tiny cogs in a fighting machine. If the machine doesn't have gas, or even one of these little cogs is missing, the fight against germs is impeded, which gives the germs time to attach to a body organ and multiply. The result can be fatal.

One would think that the primary cause of malnutrition is lack of food production, but this is not the case. In fact, virtually all countries produce enough food to feed all of their populations. The problem is more related to food distribution. The term used to describe this problem is "food insecurity," meaning a lack of access to adequate food supplies. Frequently, this lack of access means that a family cannot afford the food. In addition to an inadequate supply of food to poorer families, there may be other problems. Sometimes adult male members of the family take disproportionately large amounts of the available food or eat all of those foods that are high in vitamins and minerals (not something that makes me particularly proud of my gender). Also, frequent illnesses from contaminated water or intestinal parasites may contribute to malnutrition. Thus, a malnutrition strategy has many issues that can be addressed.

THE STRATEGY

As in every strategy of this book, you need to do considerable study before you are ready to implement a malnutrition strategy. Since malnutrition is a medical diagnosis, you should have medical backup for serious cases.

This strategy can take a DOTS approach, a community development approach, or both. DOTS ordinarily goes with tuberculosis treatment, but the concept of directly observing treatment can be used for any disease, particularly for those requiring long treatment. In a malnutrition DOTS strategy, the idea is to keep a registry of undernourished children and organize workers and volunteers so that those children get frequent attention and consistent treatment until their nutritional status has stabilized.

If you want to lean more toward community development, spend your time training community members how to choose and prepare healthy meals, keep the men from taking the larger share (good luck with that!), prevent diseases that contribute to malnutrition, etc. A hybrid between these ideas could utilize DOTS for the treatment of malnutrition, provide a track for malnutrition prevention, and utilize good community development principles (described in Chapter Thirteen) at every level.

The mainstay of treatment is to monitor and increase caloric intake. There are many ready-to-eat foods available specifically for treating malnutrition. These can be purchased by the community, secured through the World Food Program, donated from charities, or provided by a national church. However, please be careful to refer severe cases, particularly among infants, to a medical practitioner as serious problems can come from re-feeding too much too fast.

In a very restricted Muslim area, an apostolic worker made many disciples and encouraged them to make more disciples throughout their nation. One disciple raised the money to open a one-room center in a poor section of town to combat malnutrition. Women could bring their babies to be checked for weight and height and could receive help if their children were malnourished. On the day that I visited, there were more than a dozen women with their babies waiting to be seen. There were also two men from that community who were doing the work. The disciple showed me around, encouraged the workers, and demonstrated great compassion for the women and babies.

After the babies were checked, height and weight were compared against a graph to determine if each was well- or undernourished. This disciple did not live in that community and felt that the community should take ownership for the project. Therefore, she enlisted these men to volunteer their time at the clinic. Within a very short time, she had led one of these men to the Lord.

Please understand that this disciple is not well-educated or wealthy. She is only a little better off than those whom she serves and doesn't have a husband to support her. Because of the motivation of the Holy Spirit, she has effectively entered a totally unreached community and has begun to make disciples while helping the needy. If the Lord continues to draw people to Himself through this ministry, she can easily hand this project over to the new church so that they may reach the entire community for Jesus.

Besides working out of a center, an apostolic team could make house-to-house visits in a poor community, slum, or refugee camp. This act would accomplish the difficult strategy objective of *getting behind closed doors* and would be more reproducible in other communities.

Another nutrition issue is the common problem of overnutrition. Among an enormous refugee population, we were once asked to provide a free medical clinic for the needy. We only ran the free clinic for three days and on the last day, we saw so many undernourished and ill children that it broke our hearts. On the first two days, though, we saw a long line of obese women complaining mostly of knee pain. We tried to explain that the arthritis was a result of regular-sized knees being forced to carry a much-greater-than-regular-sized body. We couldn't understand why these women were so huge when the children and most of the people walking around the camp were so thin. We found out that these women were the many wives of the camp leaders. They were seen first, over two full days, because their husbands didn't allow other camp members to be seen before their wives. They were obese because these women had been taking all they wanted from the free food from humanitarian organizations before distributing to others.

These women, and many others that I have seen in more developed countries, have a weight problem. And they hate it. Just like the undernourished children, their names can be placed in a registry, and in-home visits can be made to teach them about dieting and proper nutrition.

IMPLICATIONS FOR A
CHURCH-PLANTING MOVEMENT

There are some great things about a malnutrition strategy. For one thing (as already indicated), national disciples tend to love it. The issue is so compelling that they enjoy giving their own money and time to help fatten up babies and children. I don't know of any national teams doing a diet strategy, so I can't say if they would go for that as enthusiastically. Outside apostolic teams can also enter communities effectively with the malnutrition strategy, especially if the problem is on the radar screen of the health authorities.

Families with malnourished children may minimize the problem initially. Down deep, however, they know that something is wrong and will appreciate help. Because disciple makers make frequent visits into many homes and are caring for the needy, this strategy is also good at making disciples. It has the wonderful advantage of giving actual bread *for* life while teaching about the Bread *of* life.

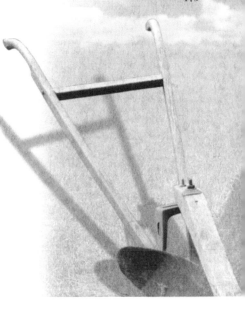

CHAPTER 18

HIV/AIDS

- Thirty-three million people are living with HIV.
- Fifty percent of HIV patients are female.
- The epidemic is moving into China and India (statistics compiled in 2007).[18]

Human Immunodeficiency Virus (HIV), the germ that causes Acquired Immunodeficiency Syndrome (AIDS), came on the scene in 1981 and has rocked the world since. Perhaps no other disease is as well-known or is so feared. It is the fourth leading cause of death worldwide and is number one in Africa.

The reason for the panic is the virulence of the germ. Just about any other infectious disease has some kind of a cure, but HIV doesn't. There are medicines that can slow down the effects of the germ but once you get HIV, you will have it until you die. For this reason, and because the manner of death is a progression through many illnesses, AIDS is scary.

THE PROBLEM

Before an HIV-infected person has the symptoms of AIDS, the virus may lie as a latent infection for years. Millions of people around the world have HIV but have no symptoms. They may not even know that they are infected. They live a normal life, even while unknowingly infecting other people with the virus.

The virus lives in human body fluids and is usually transferred from person to person through sexual intercourse, sharing of intravenous needles, or from an infected mother to her unborn baby. If we could identify and educate every HIV-infected person, we could make significant progress toward containing the virus. That goal just isn't practical and may be an infringement on personal rights. So governments keenly aware of the problem try many different techniques to slow down the spread of HIV while treating those with AIDS.

THE STRATEGY

There are two categories of people to be helped through an HIV/AIDS strategy:

1. Those who need ministry:
   a. People who know they have HIV infection but do not yet have AIDS
   b. People who are living or dying with AIDS

2. Those who need education about HIV/AIDS:
   a. People who are unaware of their HIV infection
   b. People who have the potential to be infected by HIV

As in the malnutrition strategy, the first group of people could be managed and helped through a DOTS approach. HIV and AIDS patients, as identified by local doctors, could be entered into a registry and visited regularly in their homes. An apostolic team could assure that the patient received appropriate medical care, could provide counseling, and could provide some of the same services discussed in the hospice strategy.

The second group of people could be helped through a community development approach. Volunteers in the community could be trained and could accompany the apostolic team as they visited every home to teach about HIV prevention. In small communities, the apostolic team and national disciples could provide this house-to-house service.

HIV/AIDS strategies can be used in urban or rural settings. The important factor is to have well-trained workers, preferably national disciples, who make the in-home visits and provide caring services. This team should work with a local physician so that he can offer HIV testing and so that they will have somewhere to refer people with medical problems. The team's job will mainly be to provide counseling and education, but they can also be taught how to treat some of the simple symptoms of AIDS, like fever, rashes, or pain. Remember, this counseling and education is not just for the HIV patient. The entire family is being impacted by this disease and will need attention.

In endemic areas, governments should have no objection to your workers entering every home in every community. Of course, this must be done sensitively and in cooperation with community leaders, but there are few places that will turn you away.

Because HIV infection is greatly related to sexual promiscuity in most areas, a common strategy is to teach the importance of sexual abstinence before and outside of marriage. Many countries have used the "True Love Waits" program with great success. The strength of this program is that counseling results in an offer for one to make a personal commitment by signing a pledge card.[19] The program has focused mainly on those who are not yet married, but it can be adjusted to address the issue of sexual responsibility with the whole family.

CONFIDENTIALITY

As you can imagine, the stigma associated with HIV/AIDS is huge. Since it is thought of as a disease acquired through sinful behavior, the label of "HIV patient" is seen by many as synonymous with "sinner"—a label that applies to all of us but which no one sews on his shirt. For this reason, many people are resistant to be tested for HIV. Patients who test positive do not want anyone to know about their disease. The last thing that will be welcomed is a foreigner's vehicle, which is known to visit the home of HIV patients, parked in front of the house. Therefore, every effort must be taken to keep people's HIV status confidential. Some suggestions:

- Don't use "HIV" or "AIDS" in the titles of your workers.
- Have each worker sign a document about confidentiality, and make these documents known to community leaders.
- Emphasize the education portion of the strategy so that your team will be known as visiting people to teach about HIV prevention.
- Integrate visits to HIV/AIDS patients and education visits so that the community will not know when you are visiting patients with the disease.

IMPLICATIONS FOR A
CHURCH-PLANTING MOVEMENT

Imagine being told that you have a disease that will slowly take all of your power until it finally takes your life. Imagine further that you hear this news and have no hope in Christ—no hope for encouragement from the Spirit, for peace from the Prince, and for a home in heaven. Millions of people around the world currently live in the manner I have just described. They know that they have HIV, they understand all of the implications of their diagnosis, and they are very frightened.

HIV patients realize that there is no one on this earth who can cure them. And they probably are not aware that hope through

Christ is actually quite near and obtainable. Strategies revolving around HIV/AIDS must meet people where they are and sensitively introduce them to our Hope who brings us such indescribable security.

HIV/AIDS is a condition that is related to behavior, and behavior is related to morality. You can motivate people through fear, telling them that sex outside of marriage can result in AIDS. It is a much better argument, however, and is perfectly natural to tell people that God created man and woman to be monogamous within the context of marriage. You can easily personalize this argument by giving stories of success and failure and explaining how truth, in addition to this issue of sexuality, is available through the Bible and the Holy Spirit.

As in the other strategies, the team must always press on to mobilize and empower the disciples from the harvest. These individuals can continue to utilize the HIV/AIDS strategy to enter homes in unreached areas. They can teach what they have learned and give their own testimonies of how their lives have been changed through Jesus.

CHAPTER 19

MEDICAL STRATEGIES

Enter the Community	Make Disciples	Empower the Church
✪ ✪ ✪	✪ ✪	✪ ✪ ✪

✔ URBAN ✔ RURAL ✔ DEVELOPED ✔ DEVELOPING

Many years ago, I was working with another doctor, a nurse midwife, and a veterinarian to take the Gospel to a large, unreached people group. I spoke the business language to some degree, but the vast majority of people were nonliterate mountain folk who only spoke the indigenous language.

Our team was inexperienced in church planting, but we knew enough to use the book of Acts as our guide. We also had a clear vision of indigenous churches multiplying throughout the region. Beyond an understanding of our starting and finishing points, we had no idea how to get from where we were to where we wanted to go.

It seemed logical to us that the best place to make disciples in this closed culture would be inside homes. We had hosted medical clinics in schools or clinics in the past and realized that these did not provide a good venue for teaching about Jesus. We went to the district health officer for permission to visit each home for the purpose of teaching the people how to stay healthy. He greatly appreciated our offer to help but stated that the Muslim culture did not allow foreign men to enter into their homes. He then requested that we provide free medical services from some of his abandoned clinics in the mountains. This suggestion was not what we wanted to hear, but we felt obligated to submit to his request since he was the health authority over the area. And we had a little plan up our sleeves that we hoped would work out.

For the next six months, we saw thousands of patients and gave away thousands of dollars in medicines. We were able to pray for patients in the name of Jesus, but the makeshift clinics kept us busy, leaving no opportunities to preach the Gospel. We pushed our team and national volunteers very hard and won a great reputation for ourselves. We called this phase of our work "getting slaughtered for Jesus" because we worked long hours under very difficult conditions. Everyone came to know our vehicles in the mountains and recognized us as we walked around town.

When we felt the time was right, we went back to the district health officer. We explained that our work was not really improving the lives of the people because they were not learning how to prevent the diseases plaguing their lives. We asked to stop the medical clinics in order to teach the people about disease prevention. Because of our hard work and reputation, the district health officer agreed to this plan and helped us arrange schools and mosques where we could teach.

Of course, we knew that we could not effectively teach about health or the Gospel in these venues either, but we knew that teaching the people was one step closer to our goal. We intentionally taught in a didactic manner, standing over the people using complicated charts. Dr. Josh would point to a diagram and say, "The eggs of Ascaris lumbricoides enter the gastrointestinal tract through the oral orifice and descend the esophagus and stomach into the duodenum." People would stare blankly at us, accept a free bar of soap, and would leave quietly. We planned to fail at this stage, and we failed successfully for about three months.

We returned to the district health officer and told him of our repeated failure. The people, we explained, had never been to school and could not learn from our lectures. He understood completely and recommended that we give up. At this point, we made our move.

"Perhaps," we offered, "if we went into each home, with the husband and wife present, we could show each family how to keep themselves healthy. Of course, we could also attend to medical problems at the same time."

"This is a great idea," he exclaimed and gladly gave us permission to do the same thing that he had said was not allowable nine months earlier.

From that day, we began visiting in homes. We saw the sick and taught families how to prevent disease. We were able to present the Gospel, make disciples, and form house churches.

I have intentionally put this strategy toward the end because this book is primarily for apostolic workers with no background in medicine. Having the right kind of medical professional on your team, however, can be a great benefit. I say "the right kind," because there are many of us doctors who are the wrong kind. As I have already stated, the right kind of medical professional is just like any other disciple. They have a teachable heart and surrender everything to Jesus Christ, including the profession of medicine. They are completely pliable under the influence of God and are flexible to fill roles that many medical professionals would see as beneath them. This kind of medical disciple is rare, but you will find that God is powerful and has even molded some doctors into His servants.

For our purposes, I am making a distinction between *health strategies* and *medical strategies*. The category of *health strategies* is broad and covers everything related to water, food, shelter, sanitation, disease prevention, and health care. With the exception of the rehabilitation strategy, the health strategies to this point have not required any training in medicine or any background in health. Medical strategies, though, are a sub-category of health strategies and do require at least one team member who has been medically trained. (The rehab strategy, requiring evaluative visits by a rehab expert, really is a medical strategy, but I positioned it after Luke 10 and hospice because of its similarity to those strategies.)

MEDICAL STRATEGY POSSIBILITIES

Medical strategies can meet many different needs. I hate to repeat myself, but the way to use a medical strategy is to first determine what is needed for church planting and then insert the medical strategy necessary to reach those objectives. If you have a cardiologist on your team, or you are a cardiologist, do not construct a strategy around cardiology. That would be going at it backwards, looking for needs that fit your resources rather than being God's resources that fill strategic needs. Evaluate the status of church planting among your people, determine what has been preventing them from receiving the Gospel, and then use your cardiology resources, if applicable, to overcome that barrier. If cardiology services are not the absolute best ingredient to move your team toward church-starting objectives, have the cardiologist practice house-to-house primary care, teach disease prevention, evangelize, prayerwalk, or wash dishes. Apostolic ministry is not about us; it is about His glory.

CLINIC-BASED STRATEGIES

Medical strategies can be institution, clinic, or mobile based. Institution-based strategies are covered in their own chapter, so let's look at clinic-and mobile-based strategies.

A clinic-based strategy can operate out of its own building, tent, government clinic, schoolhouse, community center, or doctor's house. The point is that a clinic-based strategy is seen by the community as an established place where medical services can ordinarily be found at set hours. They are just like institution-based strategies but are smaller in all ways. The buildings are smaller, are open for fewer hours, and perform fewer services.

As you can readily see, these strategies are strong on some of the ABCs and are weak on others. They can be great for accessing unreached areas, particularly in developing countries, but they can be weak in getting behind closed doors. One must do everything possible to work on this aspect of the strategy. It *can* be done with the right design.

For example, a physician in Northern Africa lived in a small, rural community and operated a clinic there. Without the clinic, foreigners would not have been allowed to live in such a remote region; the clinic was necessary. The doctor, however, limited his hours at the clinic so that he could spend the needed time visiting in homes and sharing the Gospel through Bible stories.

When the village religious leader realized what was going on, he went to the Islamic council to stop the doctor and the new disciples from working in the area. The religious leader's wife said she wanted the doctor's work to continue and for her daughters to be taught about Jesus. To emphasize her position, she threatened to withhold her affections from her husband if he did not stop harassing the doctor. He was convinced by her argument and allowed the doctor and his team to continue the work. The team shared boldly and saw the Lord do many remarkable things. Disciples multiplied and churches reached out to take the Gospel to very remote communities. This same approach could be used with any primary care physician, nurse practitioner, or physician's assistant.

Surgeons and dentists can also be used in clinic-based strategies if they can temper their passion for high-tech clinical practice and primarily be disciple makers. It is imperative that they provide competent surgical care, but they should not invest too much in technology above the local standard. Surgeries should be confined to outpatient procedures, and complicated cases should be referred to a government institution. It is all right for a surgeon to occasionally follow his patient to the hospital and perform or assist in the surgery. This act can be a great demonstration of compassion to the patient's family and entire community. But the doctor must see every surgical case as an opportunity to get into the home of a needy family to share the Gospel. If he begins to invest more in surgery than in disciple making, I believe he will have greatly decreased his relevance to God's agenda.

If a surgeon or dentist works with proficiency, he quickly can provide a reputation of credibility for the team. A team providing surgery or dental services is much more likely to survive the scrutiny of community authorities, but this should not be exchanged for disciple making. The hallmark for all medical practitioners is that they see their primary task as making disciples and use medical practice as a healing tool that helps to achieve that objective.

In practice this means that the practitioner will demonstrate the most passion about making disciples and will adjust daily work so that it has the greatest amount of overlap with disciple making. He will spend much of medical practice time teaching others how to perform simple procedures, treat common diseases, and prevent disease. He also will follow up on patients by going into their homes. The majority of time will position the practitioner to make disciples and empower the church.

MOBILE-BASED STRATEGIES

The strength of medical practice is its ability to reach into almost any community and to provide sustained access to that community. Commonly, apostolic workers will tell us that an area of their country is off limits to foreigners, but when medical personnel visit, the minister of health will beg us to work in those same areas to provide medical services.

Therefore, medical personnel can be used to open up communities that are wary of outsiders. When it is absolutely necessary, a small permanent clinic can be an option, but many small communities can be accessed through mobile medical clinics. These small communities include slums in an urban setting or refugee camps.

In mobile clinics, everything needed is loaded into a hardy vehicle and driven to unreached communities. These communities have been identified as those that are otherwise inaccessible and that have asked for medical services. It is necessary to limit the number of patients seen per day as word of the clinic may spread up and down the highway, and van loads of patients can arrive late in the day. Registering the names of only a limited number of people is wise. Doctors should prioritize compassion over numbers as it is impossible to see everyone.

If the people are more open to the Gospel, you should choose small communities to provide medical services house to house. You may be able to visit every house in a few weeks. You will see patients much more slowly but will be able to share the Gospel with a few families every day.

Remember that making disciples entails not only putting yourself in an environment that is conducive to sharing about Jesus, but also being before an audience who sees you and your team members as people of great integrity. People should be impressed that you have come to them with help services and great compassion, but they should also be impressed by the level of care received. Medical services should be delivered by those who are competent and qualified. Be honest about the training of your personnel and stick to those medical arenas for which each of you are trained. A pediatrician can give a general opinion about a gynecological problem, but he must emphasize that this is not his area of expertise and should refer the patient to someone who is qualified.

Mobile medical and dental clinics can be effective if used correctly. The most common mistakes are to prioritize medical care over the making of disciples and to move on too quickly. Stay in a community for long periods of time, perhaps visiting a few communities each week for many months, healing the sick, and making disciples. By this time you should see the Lord do great things. If there is no evidence that the Lord is working among the people after months of work, move on to other communities or alter your strategy. Continually ask this question, "How many people heard the Gospel this month in this community?" In some areas, the barriers are so overwhelming that large numbers may not be possible in initial stages. You cannot make disciples on your own, but with God's help, you can advance the Gospel. God does not bring people into His kingdom without that component.

OTHER USES OF MEDICAL PERSONNEL

Medical personnel can be helpful with the implementation of any of the other health strategies discussed thus far. Remember, those strategies do not provide medical services, but having medical personnel gives credibility to the team and will give you confidence. A DOTS strategy does not require a doctor or nurse, but such a person on your team would help you learn about DOTS much more quickly and could be the liaison with the WHO and government authorities.

In the same way, a Luke 10 strategy can benefit by having a medically trained person on the team. In Northern India, a church-planting team with a nurse was heart broken over a friend with tuberculosis. She had been discharged from the hospital because of the apparent hopelessness of her case. After prayer, the team decided to bring the woman into their home where they could give her the correct medications and pray for her. She recovered from the TB and came to faith with her husband. The team learned from this and added this practice to what they were doing. Team member Scott wrote:

> The medical team took on another in-house patient, which led to his conversion to Christ. This eventually became a regular practice of the team, to take on patients who were without hope to live at the center for a while, eventually nursing them back to health and leading them to Christ.
>
> ... the care of the medical team, the love and friend-ship of the believers, and praying for the sick would prove to be the key ingredients that won the majority of the church members to the Lord.

Scott also gave some examples of how the team not only used the medical skills of their nurse but utilized the power of prayer to heal:

> ... men prayed for the sick and saw many powerful miracles.

... the baby had not moved in almost two weeks. They had been to the local government maternity hospital where they were told that the baby was dead and would have to be aborted. Dhan Singh simply laid his hands on Chandra Bahadur's wife and prayed a simple prayer. The baby began to kick and move again. Chandra Bahadur and his family gave the glory to Jesus, believed, and took baptism.

Karan Bahadur was sick with tuberculosis. Finally, in the middle of the night, his breathing stopped. His wife ran out of the house screaming that he was dead, and all the neighbors came and confirmed that Karan was indeed dead. In spite of this, Karan Bahadur's wife ran to Bhim Bahadur's house and brought him to where her husband's body lay. Bhim Bahadur laid his hands on Karan and prayed a simple prayer. Immediately, Karen began breathing and became conscious. He said he felt extremely hot and asked someone to fan him and get him some water to drink. We do not know if Karen was medically dead. Whatever happened, it was a tremendous testimony to the power of God. Karan believed in Jesus and began to lead others to Christ through his witness.

Also around this time, Bhim Bahadur introduced Scott to his neighbor, Therlok Sharma, a high-caste Bhojpuri from Bihar state who worked as a carpenter. One day, Therlok brought a friend to Scott's house. His friend, Kamleshwar Sharma, was having severe abdominal pain. Scott had one of the medical team examine him and give him some medication, but the pain remained. Later an itinerant Nepali evangelist and some of the members of the church prayed for him, and he was healed. Scott followed up with him and began a Bible study for Therlok and Kamleshwar; both confessed faith in Jesus. They also introduced

Scott to other high-caste Bhojpuris, for whom he prayed and saw some healings. Several others from this group believed, and they burned their idols.[20]

This team admitted serious shortcomings in language ability but in a short time, their work resulted in over 95 baptized disciples in several indigenous house churches in an area hostile to the Gospel. Their method was simple. They cared passionately for the hurting, used what medical abilities they had to nurse the hopeless back to health, and prayed for the power of Jesus to heal. Because they were faithful to God, He was faithful to them and added to their number. Scott's poignant summary of their experience tells it all: "We have seen how the Lord Himself has used us like tools in the hands of a skilled mason." A beginning built on faith, compassion, and prayer could easily be the spark that ignites a powerful disciple-making movement, just as we saw in the book of Acts.

HOME HEALTHCARE

In the old days, a cancer patient was admitted to a hospital and waited hours for the nursing staff to insert an IV for his medicine, which dripped in very slowly. Then more paperwork had to be done so that the patient could be discharged, only to repeat the process for all subsequent treatments. Each treatment took most of the day and cost a bundle.

Decades ago the idea of *home healthcare* was established. With this model, a cancer patient can stay at home for most care. A nurse performs the same services in a much more comfortable environment, taking much less time and charging considerably less than a bundle. This method works not only for cancer patients but for those with all manner of maladies. The rehabilitation strategy (previously discussed) is based on the home healthcare model.

Nevertheless, home healthcare is not common in many countries of the world or is in early stages of development. Because it is a medical strategy, home healthcare requires medical personnel to perform the services. The potential is there for home healthcare to be a great access tool, even in developed countries, and it can fund itself. In fact, if one can come up with the start-up capital, this strategy can eventually make a sizable profit.

IMPLICATIONS FOR A
CHURCH-PLANTING MOVEMENT

Western healthcare is the international standard. Few disciplines rival its acceptance in even the most closed areas of the world. It provides access not only to restricted areas but sustained access so that medical teams can stay in restricted areas for long periods of time. Medical strategies do have the capacity to get workers behind closed doors on multiple visits, but this objective must be pursued with great intentionality.

It may be a bit more difficult for national families to relate to Western medical personnel than to community development workers, and many of the families that are visited are not quite as hurting as in the rehab and hospice strategies. Therefore, disciple making may be somewhat less effective than in some other strategies.

As for empowering the church, unless you have medical personnel among your disciples, this strategy does not transfer to nationals. Instead, it can be an effective tool for mobilizing disciples into new communities and homes. These disciples can be translators or medical assistants. They should be sent back to homes to make sure visited patients are doing better or to answer any questions about what the doctor said. At that point, effective disciple making can take place.

All in all, medical strategies can be an excellent way to engage an unreached people group. Keep in mind that doctors are not generally church-planting strategists. It is up to you to design a strategy that follows the ABCs and teach the strategy to your medical personnel. By working together as a body, you should be able to do great things for the Lord. If the doctors want to do it their own way, just fire them!

CHAPTER 20

TRADITIONAL BIRTH ATTENDANTS

Enter the Community	Make Disciples	Empower the Church
✪ ✪ ✪	✪	✪ ✪

○ URBAN ✔ RURAL ○ DEVELOPED ✔ DEVELOPING

- A woman in Niger has a one in seven chance of dying in childbirth during her life.
- Childbirth deaths are 2,000 percent more common in Afghanistan than in the U.S.[21]
- Untrained Traditional Birth Attendants (TBAs) deliver the majority of babies in the developing world, usually in the delivering mother's home.

Women have been having babies a long time, but things can still go wrong. This is especially true in the developing world where many factors make the delivery of a baby a risky business. Ideally, to decrease that risk, every delivery should be attended by a skilled worker with appropriate equipment available in the event of a complication. Yet, the majority of humankind does not live in an ideal world.

THE PROBLEM

All over the developing world, traditional birth attendants are the only alternative to having one's baby with no attendant. The TBA is generally a servant of the community who may have inherited the job from her mother without formal training. This lack of training makes her a risk to the natural delivery process, but also makes her frustrated with the job. Of course she wants to be successful in the work and see healthy deliveries.

THE STRATEGY

A traditional birth-attendant strategy has one big limitation. Rather than working with many people in a community, this strategy only works with one—the TBA. If she becomes a disciple through your interaction with her, she will carry the Gospel from house to house in a community. If this is your only strategy and if you are working with only one TBA who does not become a disciple, you have traveled fully into a strategic cul-de-sac.

On the other hand, community TBAs are already entering into homes on a regular basis. By winning many community TBAs to Christ, you have the potential to end up with a church planter in each of these communities. My point is that you need to make some decisions about when to choose the TBA strategy. For example, this strategy focuses entirely on women. You should consider this strategy only when you have a female team member who has the capacity to enter the community and make disciples.

A TBA strategy doesn't have to stand alone. Female team members can enter the community with a TBA strategy accompanied by male team members who may be doing a community development strategy. Creative teams use these strategy ideas for brainstorming and before entering into concerted prayer. In this manner, they create their own strategies based upon the leading of the Holy Spirit.

A strength of the TBA strategy is that it is often highly valued in certain parts of the world. An incarnational team that is teaching traditional birth attendants can frequently drive with ease through checkpoints and is welcomed into even the most restricted communities. If the maternal and child mortality rates are high among the people group with whom you are working, everyone will recognize the importance of your work and will appreciate you. You will enter the community with integrity.

STEPS IN A TBA STRATEGY

Modern midwifery is a difficult field requiring years of study, but we aren't talking about modern midwifery. In many areas where I have worked, the delivery practices actually contribute to disease. Rather than letting a natural process take place, TBAs have told me about various scary interventions that they were taught and which they practice. Your goal is to become aware of the current practices and do your best to improve them. Any improvement can be considered as success.

Although one does not need to be a doctor, nurse, or midwife to train TBAs, personal study is necessary. Much of the material can be learned over the Internet or from textbooks, but it also would be advisable to spend many hours with a local obstetrician or trained midwife to get ideas as you develop your training curriculum. Topics to be understood are:

1. Antenatal care
2. Labor and delivery
     a. Preventing infection
     b. Minimizing blood loss
3. Neonatal resuscitation
4. Postpartum care

A great place to begin your study is at the USAID Global Health eLearning Center at www.globalhealthlearning.org.

Many of these strange words can be intimidating, but a few weeks of study should make you comfortable with each of these subjects. After you or a team member feels confident with home deliveries, you need to have a discussion with community leaders about their practices regarding midwifery. Ask many questions. What does a woman usually do when it comes time for her to deliver? How many women deliver at home? Is the community satisfied with this system? If they use TBAs, what kind of training do they receive? Are any women or children ever lost in childbirth? Also ask the birth attendant many questions. If all goes well and the TBA is eager to be trained, it is time to start training.

According to studies in Africa and Asia, the training of TBAs has been shown to decrease infant deaths but has not been shown to decrease maternal deaths. That doesn't mean that you should give up on that part of the training. Remember, the objective is to spend as much time as possible with the TBA, making her into a strong disciple. This added training can still save a woman's life. People beat statistics every day.

IMPLICATIONS FOR A
CHURCH-PLANTING MOVEMENT

Perhaps the most beautiful explanation of our new life in Christ was given to Nicodemus one night as he spoke to Jesus. He was told, "Unless someone is born of water and the Spirit, he cannot enter the kingdom of God. Whatever is born of the flesh is flesh, and whatever is born of the Spirit is spirit" (John 3:5b-6).

A TBA who is a disciple of Christ will attend the delivery of water, in which a child of flesh is born in a healthy manner. With the help of the Holy Spirit, she will also attend the delivery of Spirit, in which members of her community are born again, by the Spirit, into the family of God. If she is a disciple, she will be a disciple maker. Furthermore, her progeny of the Spirit can also be disciple makers.

Do you see how easily an incarnational team could use this strategy to enter dozens of communities, go back to each community four to six times, and go into TBA homes for an hour on each visit? Also, it could be used as a secondary strategy to add credibility to another idea. If the incarnational team were utilizing DOTS, for example, but needed more contact in a particular community, the team could consider training a TBA in that community. It is an easy *add-on* that should be considered if you live in a place in need of this service and if your team has a female disciple maker.

Dr. De was a veterinarian using health strategies to make disciples among an unreached Muslim people group. During the stage of entering the community, Dr. De was gathering information from men in a rural community when he asked the question, "Who delivers the babies here?" When he was told that this practice was performed by the village midwife, he asked to meet her. In this culture, it is somewhat unusual for a woman to be introduced to a man in this manner, but since Dr. De was a qualified health worker, the woman was brought forward.

"How long have you been a midwife?" Dr. De asked after greeting the woman.

"All of my life," she answered. "I was trained by my mother who was the village midwife before me."

"Do women or children in your care ever die?" he asked.

"Yes," she responded anxiously. "It is common here and everywhere in this region."

"Would you like to receive some training that could help you save the lives of more women and children?" Dr. De asked.

"This is what I have prayed for all of my life," the woman answered. "I am illiterate and have never been properly trained in my job. Of course I want to do a good job and don't want anyone to die or suffer. Can you teach me?"

Dr. De began teaching the community midwife through a translator until she understood how to deliver babies safely. He left her community and returned over one month later.

"Have you delivered many babies since I saw you last?" Dr. De asked the midwife.

"Yes," she said. "I have delivered several, and I have never had a better experience. I know exactly what to do with confidence. No one has died or has even gotten sick. Now I know I can do my job well."

Then Dr. De completely changed the subject. "Has anyone ever told you about Jesus Christ?" he asked.

"No," the midwife responded. "Who is this?"

So Dr. De and the translator spent a considerable time telling her the entire Gospel and explained who Jesus was and why He died for our sins. He personalized the Gospel and explained why she needed Jesus. Then he asked her, "Do you believe that this is true?"

"Dr. De," she said sincerely, "everything you say is true."

She gave her life to Jesus on that day and shared the Gospel with her family who also believed. Over the coming months, she reported to Dr. De how she was sharing Jesus with families as she went about her job as the community midwife.

CHAPTER 21

INSTITUTION-BASED STRATEGIES

Enter the Community	Make Disciples	Empower the Church
✪ ✪ ✪	✪	✪

✔URBAN ✔RURAL ✔DEVELOPED ✔DEVELOPING

The debate over the need for institution-based apostolic strategies has been around for a few hundred years now. Early medical missionaries, such as Peter Parker of Canton and John Scudder of Ceylon, believed strongly in institutions. Other early medical missionaries, such as Hudson Taylor of China and David Livingstone of Central Africa, did not base out of institutions.

Looking back on the centuries of institution-based strategies, we also find a mixed picture. There are some institution-based strategies around the world that have produced thousands of disciples, even church-planting movements, but there are many that have worked for decades producing little or no church at all. However, we have to be fair. In those places where institutions have not produced disciples, other apostolic workers have generally had the same lack of results. On the surface, it is tough to say whether or not institutions are a good or bad idea when the objectives are disciple making and church planting.

ONE SIDE OF THE ISSUE

As you might imagine, I do have an opinion on this subject, and it is based on the ABCs of health strategies. Institution-based strategies are not the norm for disciples of Jesus. Remember the very first lesson found in the Luke 10 strategy. Jesus sent us out, two by two, to preach and to heal. The problem with institutions is that the design is antithetical to this philosophy. Rather than helping disciples go out to the people, they keep disciples in one place and ask the people to come. It's sort of like the modern movement of institutional churches. Rather than "go and tell," they ask people to "come and listen."

Another problem with institutions is that they are usually not good at getting disciple makers behind closed doors. Because so many people are sick and the institution exists to serve the ill, it just doesn't seem right for institutions to close early so that the doctors and nurses can go out to share the Gospel. As in most of the mission hospitals that I have visited, the staff wants very much to get into home healthcare, but they don't have the personnel resources to do that. Too many people need surgery and medical care.

Institutions are excellent at caring for the needy, but the set-up is not practical to make disciples. An institutional strategy can't really empower the church as that would require making disciples into healthcare providers. Even then, the strategy doesn't mobilize these disciples into homes. In most cases, institutions are for healers but are not for disciple makers who strive to *preach and heal.*

THE OTHER SIDE

In some situations, however, our option as apostolic workers was to begin with an institutional approach or not begin at all. I know of several examples in which the only way for Westerners to have had sustained access into a nation was by working in institutions. Some of these were national institutions and in some situations, the government asked the Westerners to build a hospital or permanent medical clinic.

When an institutional approach is the only option, it is worth a try. Be sure to watch for typical pitfalls because the general tendency for institutional strategies is to advance into a strategic cul-de-sac. The first of these pitfalls has to do with expectations. As people begin to dream about an institution, they frequently get led down the path of "bigger and better." Since they love the people they are trying to reach, they want them to have the best. This translates into an attempt to bring a higher standard of medical care to the community. After all, if people in the West can have great medical care, the people who we are caring for should at least have something comparable.

This thought is a major move toward the mind of a healer and away from the mind of a disciple and disciple maker. We are not trying to transform the community through better healthcare but rather to transform the community through the power of the Holy Spirit. Remember the strategy of the book of Acts. They entered the community, they made disciples, and they empowered the disciples, which included getting out of there quickly. It is right for practitioners to do their absolute best. Incompetent or negligent medical practice, in any context, is a sin. But remember the story of Peter and John healing the paralyzed man? After the healing, it took Peter only three sentences to begin talking about Jesus and by the end of the day, the Gospel had spread throughout the city. Your objective as a disciple maker is to quickly use your medical platform as a means to produce an empowered church. Your goal is to be there only as long as this takes. Attempting to raise the standard of healthcare for the area, especially by filling the institution with modern equipment, is counterproductive to this objective and this goal.

Related to this is the issue of the building itself. If you build a building, you obviously expect to stay for a long time. If you expect to get the disciple-making job done and move on quickly, you will go with a national institution or with whatever is available. If the government asks you to build a building, I would not give in. I would explain that you do not plan to make this new nation your home. The wise thing would be to teach your skills to national doctors and empower them to do the best possible work within their existing healthcare system. (Remember that all of this discussion is within the context of an area that can only be accessed through medical institutions.) This method perpetuates good health practices in the country and is more conducive to disciple making. Your home is in heaven and after planting reproducing churches among all nations, we will be able to settle down there.

The second pitfall is loss of vision. I have been over and over this, but I don't think it can be stated too often. The vision is a movement of disciples who are multiplying across the nation. If you do not write this above your doorpost and have it tattooed to your forearm, you may well be one of the many who slowly migrates toward a vision of only helping sick people in the name of Jesus. Running hospitals and clinics is easier than making disciples and quickly produces exciting stories about someone who was helped. You must determine that your measure for success is the number of people who have heard the Gospel and the number of disciples made per month—not the number of physical cures.

The third pitfall is to overvalue the institution. Let's suppose a farmer bought a tractor. From the very beginning, his tractor did wonderful things that he had never seen before. It plowed up the ground and made it much easier to get out the rocks. It also harrowed the field and made the soil perfect for planting. Of course, the tractor also broke down from time to time. Nonetheless, when the farmer wasn't fixing his tractor, he could be found sitting high in the seat riding back and forth over his field. Sadly, because the farmer never planted any seeds, he had no crop that year, and his family almost starved to death.

Institutions are like tractors. If they help us bring in a larger crop in a shorter amount of time, they are good tools. If they do not help us bring in a crop or if they slow down crop production, they are bad tools, and we must throw them away. And let me warn you, if you spend a lot of money on a tool such as a tractor, it will be very difficult to throw away if it does not prove to be the fastest way to bring in a harvest. Don't allow yourself to fall in love with, or become obligated to, the tool. We must be in love with and obligated to the harvest, because this is what our Lord cares about.

Years ago we were taking the Gospel to a new region with medical/dental backpacking teams. There was a traditional church in the region that had not grown in over 100 years. The church had a building with a steeple and even had a little Christian school in the middle of the Buddhist city. Each year, on our way to the rural areas, we dropped by the church to see the pastor who welcomed us warmly and prayed for us.

Everything went fine as long as we had no conversions. One year, we worked on our strategy a bit and made the first disciples. Immediately the authorities tried to find out who was responsible. Since we had already left the area, they went to the pastor of the church and asked questions. They told him that if *we* continued this evangelical activity, they would revoke *his* charter for the school and the church building. The pastor, who really was a wonderful man, sent word to us that we were not to return to the area. He wanted to reach the 400,000 people in the rural areas but not at the risk of losing his institutions.

"The other side" is supposed to be listing good things about institution-based strategies, but mostly pitfalls have been discussed. But if these pitfalls are avoided, and there is no other way to get into a country, it could be advisable for disciple makers to base out of institutions for disciple making. They must negotiate with the authorities to get rights to visit patients in their homes and to develop home-care services. The goal is the same for other strategies—for dozens of nationals to hear the Gospel each month in the beginning stages and for this number to increase above 100 or so after the first disciples are made. There are examples of disciple movements resulting from institution-based strategies, but in these cases the disciple-making team worked continually to follow the ABCs of good strategy.

LAST THOUGHTS

Years ago my family visited a 35-year-old mission hospital during their Sunday evening worship service. One of their apostolic doctors spoke that night and gave a rather sad message. He recounted the large numbers of apostolic workers who had been at the hospital, and all of the money and work that had been put into their ministry, and he pointed out that they still had not produced a national church for Jesus Christ. He labeled this as a failure and expressed his wish for their work to result in multiplying disciples.

A few days later, I was with my friend, Ed, an apostolic worker who had actually been in this difficult country for 40 years. I told him about the sermon. "Well, that is one way of looking at it," he responded. "But I'll never forget the miracles that God did 35 years ago to establish that hospital." There was another way to look at it.

Is church planting up to us or to God? I have seen apostolic workers make arguments for both answers. Some have insinuated that success in disciple making is completely related to our strategies and work. Others have told me that what we do is irrelevant, and God starts disciple-making movements among people when He wants to, regardless of our efforts. Most of us, however, especially those who are students of the New Testament, realize that we work together with God in this enterprise. We don't know what He will do or when, so we obey His command to make disciples. We expect Him to do those "God things" that He does so well.

In any given people group, if 1,000 people hear the Gospel, it is likely to result in disciples. If we put the seed of the Gospel into the soil of 1,000 hearts, we offer God an opportunity to initiate that spiritual photosynthesis that results in the miracle of growth. We are not good stewards of our time and God's money when we invest in strategies that are not likely to get the Gospel to large numbers of people.

At the same time, God has called our predecessors, and perhaps our contemporaries, to strategies of which we may not be aware. So I believe it is very wrong to pass judgment on the methods of others. I write this book for you to gain insight into good and logical strategy development based on my interpretation of Scripture coupled with my study and experience. Please do not fault anyone who sees things differently, and please forgive me if you find me to be wrong.

CHAPTER 22

DISASTER RELIEF

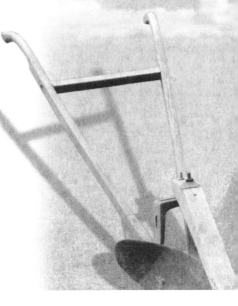

Enter the Community	Make Disciples	Empower the Church
⭐ ⭐ ⭐	⭐ ⭐ ⭐	⭐ ⭐ ⭐

✓ URBAN ✓ RURAL ✓ DEVELOPED ✓ DEVELOPING

"Gentlemen, tomorrow we will be arriving at the disaster site. We do not know where we will sleep, where we will get food or water, or where we will go to the toilet. All we know is that tens of thousands have died, more than 100,000 are homeless during a cold winter, and none of these people have had the opportunity to hear about Jesus. Are there any questions?"

We were packed in a small hotel room, and I was addressing more than 20 retired men who had left their homes with just a few days' notice to respond to a terrible earthquake. I couldn't believe that they had no questions, and I heard many men say things like, "Yep. That's about what we expected," or, "We'll be just fine. The Lord will take care of us." True disciples are awesome!

The next day, we arrived at the disaster site. I had never seen anything like it before. Every building was damaged and most flattened. People dug in the rubble trying to find their belongings. The goods were useless, but they had been of value and were all that the survivors had left. The government even had difficulty coaxing the people to the newly erected tents, because they refused to leave these small piles of broken and worthless goods.

With gratitude from the national authorities, the team of retired men set up tents, cook stoves, and a water filtration unit. Within hours, hot coffee and meals were being served.

An underground pastor we knew traveled with us. As we served the hungry and investigated other ways that we could help, he made phone calls to the disciples in the capital. Within days many of them had taken leave from their jobs to help.

Over the next several weeks, teams of relief workers gave out free food and coffee. However, without any forewarning, a government official said that our services were no longer needed. They were returning to their policy of banning outsiders from the country, and we would have to leave within the week. So much had been accomplished and plans had been made to help with construction, rehabilitation, and disciple making. These plans were swept away at once.

Then the national disciples approached us. "What are you planning to do with the stoves and the equipment?" they asked. "We would like to carry on this ministry after you leave. You see, there is no church in this entire region, and we are committed to staying until we start the first church."

Over the next few days, these disciples quit their jobs. We moved out, and they fed the homeless and made disciples. I will say it again. True disciples are awesome!

THE SITUATION

Since the beginning of this millennium, there has been one disaster after another. Wondering what God was up to, I took out a map and put a star over each recent disaster. The stars stretched across Northern Africa to the Pacific Ocean, straight through the middle of the most restricted and unevangelized part of the earth. For security reasons, it is better not to mention the specific places, but people groups who had been off limits for decades were suddenly asking for help from outsiders. Because their lives had been torn apart, they were much more open to meeting Jesus. One disaster was actually in the same city that my family had been expelled from years before.

Disaster relief is not simple. The first complicating factor is the huge number of relief workers who come to help. Dozens of agencies, with hundreds of workers from all over the world, can be found at most disasters. I have been on a plane with Mexicans, Pakistanis, French, Dutch, Cypriots, and many others as we flew into a disaster area.

Problems come with coordination. There is a special branch of the United Nations called UN OCHA—the United Nations Office for the Coordination of Humanitarian Affairs—but they frequently have a hard time managing all of these independent entities from around the world. Organizations such as Humanitarian Information Center (HIC), the Humanitarian Affairs Commission (HAC), and the Humanitarian Operations Center (HOC) are designed to facilitate humanitarian agencies, but sometimes they actually cause hindrances instead.

Besides these complications, there is one bigger problem. We never know where disasters are going to happen. When one does come along, we aren't likely to have an apostolic team in place. If a team has been in place, they end up being victims of the disaster just like the majority of the population.

On the other hand, disaster relief can be very rewarding. Several days into the earthquake disaster described, a man standing in line for food shouted, "Listen, everyone! Do you realize that these men helping us are Christians? Where are the Muslims? Why aren't they helping us?"

THE STRATEGY

Following the ABCs is important for disaster relief, because it is highly resource dependent. The disaster at the Twin Towers in New York was a heartbreaking event. Many wept and mourned for days over this tragedy. In light of all of the disasters that have occurred since, we can see that our grief is not the greatest in the world. How many hundreds of thousands have been lost since then in earthquakes, famines, wars, and tsunamis? Should we prioritize an American or Western tragedy higher, because those lost in New York were like us? I hope you realize that the answer is no. From God's perspective, the value of a tiny, nonliterate, African child is the same as that of an American PhD. In the story of the Good Samaritan, Jesus' definition of a good neighbor was someone who demonstrated mercy to the one whom no one else would help and who was not like him.

For a year or so, when there were several disasters among Muslim peoples, I kept running into a wonderful team from a large Christian relief agency. I asked how they determined when and where to respond. Their organization had a very simple guideline. They monitored CNN and responded to the top six disaster stories. Since these disasters were in the news, it assured that funding would come in to cover their work. These men did not agree with that tactic but stated flatly that it was the way it was. Because they are newsworthy and will result in more donations, new disasters in the Bible belt of America get more attention and thus higher priority than the old stories in Northern Africa and Asia, regions where those affected have a statistically negligible chance of hearing the Gospel.

Here's the point. There are disasters around the world almost always. If we use our limited personnel and financial resources on the disaster that is easiest to get to or that has the most press coverage, we will not be able to respond to those disasters among the least accessible and previously ignored people groups. On many occasions, a disaster in a closed Muslim or Hindu area is an opportunity to engage those who would otherwise be inaccessible and unreached. Saving the lives of people with our religious beliefs is a good thing, but we must not overlook the priority of using medical skills to take the love of Jesus and the Gospel into a Muslim, Hindu, or Buddhist area. God's providence may allow these disasters as an opportunity to build His church where it has never been before.

Hundreds of workers show up at disasters, some with Christian organizations. The vast majority of these workers are healers. At a huge disaster, I visited offices of three Christian relief agencies to see what they were doing. They had the usual frustrations but were persevering in the face of great difficulties to bring aid to many families.

At the end of each visit, I asked the same question: "Besides helping the people's physical needs, do you have any agenda to leave behind multiplying disciples?" In each case, I got the same response. Although they liked the idea, they did not have multiplying disciples as a goal. A few of their staff had given out a Bible or had won someone to the Lord, but that was not among their objectives. We were only able to find one team of three European families that was entering the closed Muslim area, with a population of millions, to preach and heal.

Let's go back to our ABCs. The letter "A" directs us to *access unreached areas*. The first question of strategy is whether to respond to the disaster or not. Disasters among the least reached and least accessible should be a high priority. I recommend that you establish a personal policy of committing your church to unevangelized people groups; that commitment will then guide your response to disasters rather than an inclination to go where others are going or where the cost is minimal.

The "B" of *behind closed doors* is the next step and is somewhat difficult in disaster relief, requiring serious intentionality. If you keep asking your team how you can get behind closed doors, you will come up with many ideas. You must work on this issue every day.

You also need to realize that disciple making and church planting are not done quickly in a disaster situation. It is possible to reap a great harvest, but this is a process of months rather than weeks. We must ask ourselves what kind of home visits will be appropriate and appreciated over the next months.

One idea is follow-up care for medical patients. Your team can run a medical clinic or partner with one of the medical clinics involved in disaster relief. To move to the step of getting behind closed doors, you simply need a list from the doctors of patients who would like to be visited in their homes. When visiting, show the same concern as in a Luke 10 strategy and give the patient and family time to talk. Be sure to take a small gift, and ask if you can pray for the household. Of course, this is best done with nationals as a means of empowering the church but can be done with expatriate apostolic workers, if that is all that is available.

If you have the expertise, in-home rehab also can be an excellent idea. Again, try to take nationals along and teach them to be rehab technicians. A qualified apostolic worker can oversee many national disciple makers who are working in dozens of homes.

PSYCHOLOGICAL COUNSELING

In October of 1999, a super-cyclone with wind speeds up to 180 miles per hour hit Orissa, India, and continued for three days. Twenty-feet-high tidal waves crashed eight miles inland and swept away almost everything. Over 15 million people were affected and 10,000 were killed. Thousands of villages were marooned for over two weeks before relief services arrived.

Fourteen months later, a study was done among surviving adolescents. All of these young people reported starvation and lack of treatment for physical problems. They had seen dead and mutilated bodies of people and cattle and the destruction of their homes and land.

At the time of the study, it was found that 37.9 percent of the adolescents studied were suffering from a psychological condition. The medical names for these mental illnesses are post-traumatic stress disorder, generalized anxiety disorder, and major depressive disorder. The symptoms of these disorders include nightmares, vivid flashbacks, social avoidance, decreased interest in life, feelings of guilt, suicidal thoughts, and poor performance in school.[22]

These studies are rare, but we do know that survivors of disasters in the developing world have a much greater chance of experiencing psychological damage than those in developed countries. As you can imagine, there are virtually no psychological services in most developing countries. There certainly aren't enough services for the great numbers that are affected by disasters. If the 37 percent of adolescents affected by the Orissa cyclone represent the rest of the population, millions of adults and children were psychologically damaged.

There are times when bad counseling is more damaging than no counseling. But with just a little training, anyone can be taught to be of some benefit as a counselor. The mainstay of treatment, for those who have been through trauma, is for survivors to tell their stories and express their feelings many times. It is not necessary to have answers or medicines in most cases. The main thing needed is a compassionate listener.

Psychological counseling is a great way to get behind closed doors. Just like medical follow-up and rehab, it is an excellent way to *care for the needy*, which is the "C" of the ABCs.

The "D" step, *make disciples*, does require some caution. When one suffers great loss, he goes through a grieving process. He may have disturbing dreams in which the event of loss has not occurred, only to wake up to the reality of the loss. He may be angry with the world, life, or God. He may be so remorseful that he loses all interest in life. At some point, though, the need to eat, wash, and be productive forces the griever to work toward psychological resolution.

In these early stages, it is counterproductive and rather insulting to push a "new religion" at someone. Almost everyone will appreciate personal care, encouragement, and prayer, but please resist the temptation to put evangelistic literature in care boxes or to be aggressive in evangelism. If you can be patient for just a few weeks while demonstrating Christ-like compassion, you will find a much more receptive audience to your message of hope, peace, and salvation.

Disaster relief readily lends itself to the "E" of *empower the church*. Do your best to mobilize national disciples from surrounding areas. Do not pay them a salary as this is a great opportunity for the church to step up and care for their neighbors. Instead, the best role for foreign apostolic workers is to provide structure to facilitate the relief work and disciple making.

IMPLICATIONS FOR A
CHURCH-PLANTING MOVEMENT

When Jesus was asked about the end of the age and His return, He gave this answer in Matthew 24:7-8: "For nation will rise up against nation, and kingdom against kingdom. There will be famines and earthquakes in various places. All these events are the beginning of birth pains."

I'm sure that every generation has believed that the return of Christ was near, but we know for certain that we are nearer the end than ever before. We also know that the return of Christ will come unexpectedly. As these wars, famines, and earthquakes occur, we should use even these tragedies to bring glory to the One who will return to judge the earth. It is very difficult to humble some men, but God, in His plan to redeem His remnant, seems to be using even these disasters to do just that. See what God is doing. He is opening the doors to the last remaining people groups so that they too may have access to His glory. If we are wise and mobilize the vast resources at our disposal, we can work within God's strategy to win these last groups and see the completion of the prophecy that Jesus gave in Matthew 24:14: "This good news of the kingdom will be proclaimed in all the world as a testimony to all nations. And then the end will come."

AFTERWORD

Nearly every disciple wants to be like Peter or Paul. We would love to walk with confidence into the dark places of the world, raising the ill and leaving a healthy church in our wake. But every man, without exception, is foundationally weak. We are hardly the creatures that God made us before we chose the way of sin. So our very sin nature ordinarily decides our behavior.

Remarkably, it does not have to be this way. Peter and Paul were not superhuman. We, too, have been born again, recreated by Christ Jesus, and endogenously empowered through the person of the Holy Spirit for the express purpose of good works—specifically to preach and to heal. Although we may lack confidence and training, although cultural mores and conventional wisdom may be against us, we know that we can do this, and because of our sworn pledge to obey Jesus, we know that we must preach and heal.

If we can flip that switch from a degenerate to a transformed mind, transposing our behavior from that of the first paragraph above to the second, a cascade of consequences will follow. Satan will be defeated in our lives, disciples will be made, communities will be transformed, light will replace darkness, and the rulers and powers of this dark world will retreat.

Changing the switch only requires faith. I hope this book has given you some ideas as to what *you* can do. Now, please, go in faith, preach and heal, and let us see just what *God* will do.

APPENDIX A:

STEPS OF A HOSPICE STRATEGY

Step One: Put together the hospice team

All core members of the team must be authentic disciples and must be trained in disciple making and planting of indigenous churches that multiply. If you work in an area in which there are no or few disciples, it may be necessary to add hospice team members from the majority religion of the area. These individuals would not be a part of the team's disciple-making agenda but could decrease the potential for your team being labeled as a missionary enterprise. It is also helpful to know how many weekly hours each hospice team member can contribute.

Step Two: Decide level of professionalism

Many things must be considered when making this decision. Does the term "charity" make you look like a religious entity? Does your work need a professional name? Where will funding come from? How will you handle incoming money with integrity? How do you keep everything legal? Do you need a board of trustees?

Step Three: Define parameters, vision statement, and core values

Define the parameters of the community that you will serve, write a vision statement, and determine your team's core values. After that is done, you should work on a budget for your first year. The budget should be done after you determine the parameters of your target community as transportation costs will vary with the size of the travel area.

Step Four: Train team members

Training team members and putting into place the needed medical component to provide evaluative visits and backup in case of problems are essential. Much can be learned from the Internet, doctors, psychologists, dieticians, and nurses. Some subjects that can be studied are:

1. Nutrition and exercise
2. Nonmedical pain management
3. Organization and management of medications
4. Side effects of medicines and chemotherapy
5. Managing a bedridden patient
6. Emotional support
7. Spiritual counseling
8. Family counseling
9. Issues related to terminal illnesses

Step Five: Find hospice patients
Finding hospice patients can be done through word of mouth or through advertising. At this point, the fun stuff begins.

Step Six: Assess the patient's situation
This requires an evaluative visit, some time to work out a hospice care plan, and another home visit to review this plan with the patient and family. If the patient and family agree, you move on to the step of making regular visits.

Step Seven: Make regular visits
Make home visits, as determined by the care plan. Demonstrate compassion to the patient and family, and present the Gospel.

Steps in a hospice strategy

1. Put together your hospice team.
2. Determine if you will be a charity, not for profit, or for profit.
3. Define the parameters of your target community.
4. Get training and medical backup.
5. Find hospice patients.
6. Make home evaluations.
7. Make hospice care/disciple-making visits.

APPENDIX B:

STEPS OF A REHABILITATION STRATEGY

The steps of this strategy are identical to the hospice strategy and can be church-based or done with an outside apostolic team. The program can also be a charity, a not-for-profit, or for profit entity. Once the rehab patients are identified, the strategy gets a bit more complicated.

The rehabilitation strategy requires a home evaluative visit the same way as the hospice strategy but in this case, it is more difficult as there may not be a local physical therapist or other rehab practitioner for hire. If you have a rehab person on your team, you will have no problem with this step of entering the community. Without that skill, you will have to find someone to help you. This person does not need to be a disciple, but he does need to be someone competent and dependable.

Steps in a rehabilitation strategy

1. Put together your rehab team.
2. Determine if you will be a charity, not for profit, or for profit.
3. Define the parameters of your target community.
4. Get training and medical backup.
5. Find rehab patients.
6. Make home evaluations and train technicians.
7. Make rehab/disciple-making visits.

APPENDIX C:

STEPS OF A COMMUNITY DEVELOPMENT STRATEGY

Step One: Establish your identity

Before you enter the community, you will need to put a few things in place. The first thing needed is an identity by which you can present yourself to authorities and the community. Remember, this is the identity that you present, but it is not necessarily your platform for ministry. The community will size you up and will come to conclusions about you. The identity seen is your platform for disciple making. In a good strategy, these two identities must be the same. You need simply be the person who you say you are and do the things you say you do.

You may work under the auspices of a humanitarian aid organization, a social group, a charity, or even a church. This entity should be registered in some way to satisfy local authorities when you are questioned. It is vital that the proper permissions be obtained before you set off.

Step Two: Put together your team

The team may consist of as few as two disciples, but they must be committed to the community development program. They will be visiting the community a few times each week for at least six months and cannot quit halfway through. They must also have some means of communicating to nationals. It is not necessary that these disciples have a background in healthcare, agriculture, or engineering. Professionals can be hired when needed.

This short treatise certainly does not teach you everything about community development, and your team would greatly benefit from a short training course. These classes are usually for just one or two weeks and help the team learn oral-based teaching and other skills that take some practice. Excellent training is available from Medical Missions Response (www.mmronline.org) and Equip (www.equipministries.org).

Step Three: Organize transportation and funding

This money is not to give to the community development projects but to pay for teaching materials, translators, fuel for the vehicle, etc.

Step Four: Enter the community

The principles for this step are explained in Chapter Six, Enter the Community. Choose your community wisely, based upon the criteria that you feel are important, and spend time with your person of peace and people in the community. You may want to begin your work in more than one place, but be prepared to visit each community at least twice per week. In the beginning, you will be meeting with your community contacts even more than that.

Step Five: Get a feel for community needs

A good place to start for this step is at the local school. It is very reasonable to bring in one or two doctors to screen school children so that you can determine any common illnesses. Because you have not begun your development work, and the community has not made a commitment to work with you, you can offer this as a gift to the community, although it is best to ask the community to provide the doctors. If you do bring in doctors, have the community provide their food, lodging, and all of the materials that are needed.

The school is a good place to do childhood screening, and you can bring the children forward by classes. Volunteers from the community can register each child's name, gender, age, height, and weight. The doctor should ask if the child has any chronic illness or health complaint. He should then do a quick physical exam to check for anemia, tooth decay, infections, skin problems, etc. In one community, we also asked children if a family member had died in the past year. We were surprised when several children told us that they had lost a sibling from measles.

After the screening, ask the doctor to look over the records and list any trends. Check the heights and weights against the normal levels to see if the children are undernourished or tend toward obesity. This list of problems should be shown to the person of peace and taken before the community leaders in a formal meeting.

Step Six: Establish a partnership

At this time, after you have spent much time in prayer, you will ask the community leaders if they would enter into a partnership with your team to help overcome these and other issues that they feel are important. If they are not interested, move on. There are plenty of communities that will appreciate your offer to help.

If the leaders agree, you have the option of putting together a formal board of trustees or using the community leaders for that function. In any event, it is good to invite interested and influential parties to gather so that you can explain your proposed partnership. At this point, you should explain the core values. Use stories or plays to explain these principles and ask for feedback.

You have four goals in meeting with a board or community leaders. First, you desire that they understand the program so that they will not be surprised by any aspect. If a religious leader comes to them complaining that you have taught spiritual lessons, the community leaders should defend you saying that it is part of the development curriculum. Second, this group should be prepared to solve problems, such as the one just mentioned. Third, you will ask them to introduce you to families with whom you can teach the lessons. Fourth, you want to get a commitment from them so that they will take the training to other communities.

Step Seven: Collect data

Your purpose in collecting data is to teach material that the community considers relevant. If teaching about community development is irrelevant to them, you will not get a serious audience. In the same way, you must learn about what the community values so that your Gospel presentation is relevant and communicates effectively.

In a Buddhist area, my friends performed medical and dental clinics for hundreds of villagers. They shared the Gospel, but people just shook their heads and walked off. No one was interested in the Jesus that was being preached.

None of the team spoke the language so after many unsuccessful days, they had a talk with their translators to see what they were doing wrong. "These people have no concept of the one God that you are proposing," they said. "In fact, there is no word for that God in their language. Therefore we are telling them that Lord Buddha created the heavens and the earth."

They added, "Our culture is different from your culture. We do not value the same things. Our great hope is to escape life and ascend to the nothingness of Nirvana. You are saying that followers of Jesus will obtain everlasting life and that may be good for you Westerners. But we do not want to be reincarnated over and over in this manner."

To evaluate a community, you begin by asking questions and listening. This phase is called Participative Learning and Action (PLA), and there are many PLA exercises on the Internet. These tools are simple, oral-based, and visual and are intended to gather information that is pertinent to future community development work.

For example, one PLA tool is "mapping." The objective is to define the parameters and contents of a given community as the community defines it. A group or several groups are asked to draw a map of their community. You will find that they know their boundaries and may say something like, "The people on the other side of this river are not part of our community, because they have their own well." By looking at the map, you can see where people live, where they work, where they get electricity and water, etc. In addition to mapping, an excellent tool for gathering community information is called the "Ten Seed Technique" and was developed by Dr. Ravi Jayakaran, senior director of international programs for MAP International. This is a further simplification of existing PLA techniques that provides an easy path to learn about a community's worldview. You begin by gathering a small group of people, placing 10 seeds on a piece of paper before them, and asking them to use the seeds to answer your questions. You then choose a topic and begin your investigation. Questions are asked in such a way that the answers can be represented using the seeds.

For example, you could begin researching the community situation regarding education. A first statement could be, "Use the seeds to show how many children do and don't go to school." The group will talk among themselves and will then move the seeds into groups. They may put eight seeds together representing the 80 percent of children who attend school, one seed representing the 10 percent that never attend school, and one seed representing the 10 percent that begin the school year but drop out during the harvest season.

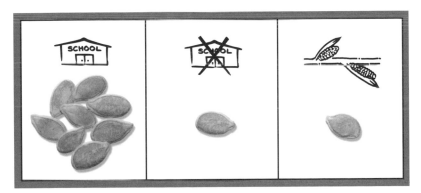

To record your information, do not write down words and numbers. This can be done in a private notebook by a recorder, but try your best to keep open information in pictures and symbols. You can record the above information by drawing a little school and drawing eight seeds by it. Another school could have an X over it with one seed beside it, and another picture could show some corn, representing harvest time, with one seed by it.

You would continue the investigation by finding out at what age children generally begin school, when girls usually drop out, when boys usually drop out, who leaves the community for further education, etc.

Ask anything that you would like, and pose the questions in such a way that the answers can be demonstrated through the use of 10 seeds. Take some time to practice this as a team, and you will quickly catch on.

The Ten Seed Technique can then be used to learn about the community's worldview. Worldview is the way in which one looks at the world. A typical American may highly value honesty and happiness. A Muslim fundamentalist may highly value honor and the struggle for personal purity. Each of these worldviews will result not only in different behaviors but in different hopes, dreams, and prayers. Dr. Jayakaran advocates the use of the Ten Seed Technique to obtain an analysis of the worldview for a community. A community's worldview may vary between men, women, children, the young, or the old, so it is wise to repeat this exercise many times with different kinds of community members, depending on the purpose for which the information is being collected. For holistic development planning, it is useful to use the community's corporate worldview.

Dr. Jayakaran has separated worldview into three essential components. These are *livelihood*, *problems*, and *uncertainties*. Information about each of these areas is determined by the Ten Seed Technique. Place the 10 seeds on a sheet of paper in front of a group from the community, and ask the group to use the seeds to show how people make a living. Without the seeds, they may list 20 different means of livelihood. The Ten Seed Technique forces them to group their ideas into the significant categories (above 10 percent) and to discard ideas that represent less than 10 percent of the community.

When they are finished, you may find that 50 percent of the livelihood comes from business, 20 percent from those having government jobs, and 30 percent are unemployed and get their livelihood from money sent to them by relatives. Record this data where everyone can see it with pictures and symbols.

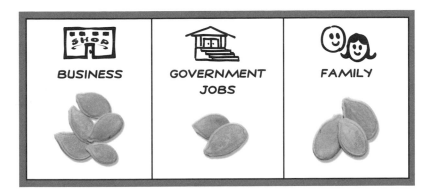

Move on by asking the group what *problems* the community faces. From this information, you may find that they are concerned with issues related to health, education, and employment. Have them use the seeds to show how important each problem is to their community.

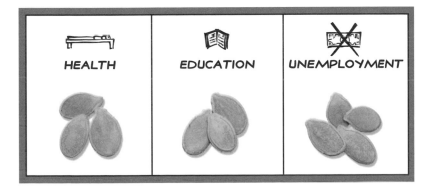

Then find out what *uncertainties* they have. This category is related to those things that they fear, which may destroy their way of life. Uncertainties may be something like loosing money to corrupt authorities or drought. If the community is rural, drought may be more important to them. A community in an urban setting, though, may prioritize the problem of corruption over the drought. It is important to remember that this will vary for each community according to their own context.

This gives you an excellent idea about what is important to the community, and you can ask many more questions about each of these categories. Find out how often droughts occur, when the drought season is, how much money people lose during a drought, etc.[23]

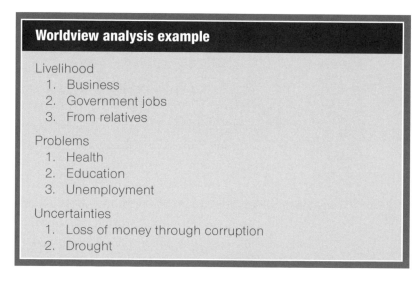

Worldview analysis example

Livelihood
1. Business
2. Government jobs
3. From relatives

Problems
1. Health
2. Education
3. Unemployment

Uncertainties
1. Loss of money through corruption
2. Drought

Step Eight: Record data

After collecting data, place these results on a pie chart (Fig. 1). The list in the above block contains three major means of *livelihood*, three main *problems*, and two *uncertainties*. This makes eight categories, so draw a circle and divide it into eight sections.

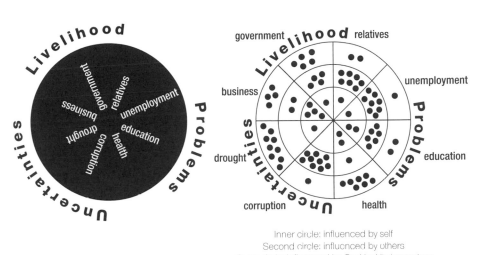

Figure 1

Inner circle: influenced by self
Second circle: influenced by others
Outer circle: influenced by God/spirits/ancestors

Figure 2

Now ask your group one question about each one of these eight categories, and record the information. The question is: "To what degree is each of these things influenced by you, others, or God/spiritual beings/ancestors?" For example, for those whose livelihood is through business, to what extent do they influence the success of their businesses? To what extent do others have an influence? To what extent does God, spiritual beings, or ancestors have an influence? You may find that your people believe that success in business is mostly up to their own work. You may find that they are largely controlled by outside human forces, or you may find that they believe that God is greatly in control of business success.

Repeat this exercise for all of the categories of livelihood, for the community's problems, and for uncertainties. Find out where they think problems and uncertainties originate. Is it their fault that they have health problems? Is the problem because a neighboring community contaminates the water? Does God send these illnesses? Do they lose money to corruption because officials are bad people or because God is punishing them? Record this information on another pie chart, as in figure 2, for everyone to see.

When you are finished, there will be a diagram, such as the one above, with 10 seeds in each of the categories of *livelihood*, *problems*, and *uncertainties*. From this fictitious example, the community believes that most things are out of their control. Lack of education and employment are seen as problems mostly brought on by others, and health problems and the uncertainty of drought are primarily in the hands of God. When you teach, witness, and pray with them, it would be good to keep these things in mind.

Step Nine: Make disciples

Remember, the step of entering the community (Step Four), lasts until you are in a place where your audience is comfortable, and you can effectively communicate the Gospel. Making disciples begins after this.

In the community development strategy, disciples can be made at several levels of the program. You will be spending much time with the person of peace and will be in his house on many occasions. You will also spend quality time with the community leadership and can easily share the Gospel with them.

If you are using volunteer community health workers (CHWs), you will be meeting with them at least weekly. In certain areas, it is possible to teach two lessons at each meeting. One of these would be related to physical, emotional, social, or moral health. The other could be related to spiritual health, and you can give oral lessons from the Bible explaining the points given earlier:

1. Where Satan and sin came from
2. How the world became cursed by sin
3. God's promise, through the prophets, to send someone to remove the curse
4. How God sent Jesus and how He proved Himself to be from God
5. How Jesus overcame the curse
6. The promise of a heaven where there is no more curse
7. What every person must do now to be saved from the curse

If it isn't possible to teach formal spiritual health lessons to the CHWs, you can visit and share in their homes or with anyone who hangs around after the training time. Eventually you will see that those CHWs who are not being drawn by the Holy Spirit will drop out of the program, but those that the Lord has His hand on will be hard workers and will bring friends who want to join the program.

The primary place where disciple making takes place, however, is inside the homes of the families being visited. You and your team can make as many home visits as you want and can share the Gospel as you go. As national CHWs come to Christ, take them with you into homes so you can model witnessing.

Step Ten: Empower the church

The community development strategy is also conducive to empowering the church because of the training structure that you have set up. Through the community development strategy, your team and national partners already will be meeting in the community and teaching in homes. As community members come to Christ, introduce them to one another so that they can gather as a church. Appoint elders and teach the ingredients, methods, and products that have been learned from studying church-planting movements (Chapter Five).

Help the church adopt methods that will allow them to reach into other communities. They can be sent out with a Luke 10 strategy and replicate the community development strategy that they have learned, use another method outlined in this book, or come up with their own strategy.

APPENDIX D:

STEPS OF A TUBERCULOSIS DOTS STRATEGY

Five key principles have been identified for a successful DOTS (Direct Observation Therapy Short-course) program:

Political commitment

Tuberculosis is more common in some places than in others, and some countries have more capacity to deal with the problem than others. If your target country has a high incidence of TB and is rather poor, the chances are good that the government is looking for outside partners to help them with this problem. The important point here is to talk to the government about how you can help with DOTS so that you will be seen as working with them.

Detection of infectious TB cases

The best way to begin is by partnering with local medical services to assure that the identified cases of tuberculosis are registered into your DOTS program. If you have the capacity, it is also possible to screen for cases of TB and refer suspected cases to the local clinic. Screening for TB can be as simple as doing a survey that asks about chronic cough or weight loss. You can work with local medical personnel on this.

Cure of infectious TB cases and prevention of drug-resistant TB

The *observation* part of DOTS comes here. Once those with tuberculosis in a community are found, the DOTS team can take their medicine to them. You should keep simple records on each patient including his weight, appetite, how much he is coughing, etc. All of these things give the DOTS team members reasons to come into homes and stay for awhile. If you are utilizing a volunteer DOTS worker in the community, spend time in his house, also, making sure that he learns these things.

Uninterrupted supply of quality TB drugs

The average patient will be taking several different medicines on a regular basis—daily or a few times each week. It is very important that the drugs used are reliable and don't run out until the end of the treatment course. If one is planning on doing this program on a big scale, there are foundations that give money for DOTS. You may be able to get money and/or drugs from them. Just make sure you don't get two months into a DOTS strategy and run out of meds.

Effective management and evaluation of the program

In some counties and remote areas, virtually nothing is being done to stop TB. Anything that you can do is an improvement—unless you were to start a program and quit a few months later. That actually would lead to more cases of drug-resistant TB and would be a bad witness for Jesus. If someone will take ownership of this program, it can be a very effective tool to get the Gospel into rural communities, refugee camps, prisons, slum areas, etc.

APPENDIX E:

WHO IS JESUS? A SHORT STORY OF THE GOSPEL

This lesson is designed to tell the entire story of the Gospel in about one hour. It is to be presented in an oral-based format (as a story) and focuses on four main points:

1. Where sin came from
2. How we became the children of Satan
3. How God adopted us into salvation
4. What will happen when Jesus returns

As an introduction, you may want to ask a question such as:

- Why do you think there is so much suffering in the world?
- Where do you think disease came from?
- Why are people so selfish?

There are several verses in the short story that you should memorize. This will give you integrity as a religious expert, and you will model to your hearers that a follower of Jesus memorizes and uses Scripture. Feel free to explain the verses after you recite them.

Part 1: Where sin came from
Before God made the world, He made thousands of angels. God is Spirit, and these angels are also spirits. They do not have bodies like people do, so they can move about between heaven and earth. But they cannot be everywhere at once like God can. They can only be in one place at a time.

God put the angels in heaven, and they worship Him and are His servants. Because God is holy and perfect, everything that He makes is perfect. Therefore, each of the angels that He made was perfect.

One of the angels created by God was named Lucifer. He was more beautiful and intelligent than the other angels, and he was given a job in authority over many other angels.

Lucifer should have loved and worshiped God like the other angels but because he was especially beautiful and intelligent, he became very proud. He wanted to become important like God, and the Bible tells us that he thought in his heart: "I will ascend to the heavens; I will set up my throne above the stars of God. I will sit on the mount of the [gods'] assembly, in the remotest parts of the North. I will ascend above the highest clouds; I will make myself like the Most High" (Isaiah 14:13-14).

When Lucifer had this thought, he was not worshiping God but was thinking of himself as great. Actually, he was worshiping himself. This pride was the first sin, and it was a great sin against God.

Many people ask, "If Lucifer was created perfect, how could he sin against God? Did God cause him to sin?" These are good questions, but the answer is very simple. Listen again to the things that Lucifer thought: "I will ascend to the heavens; I will set up my throne above the stars of God. I will sit on the mount of the [gods'] assembly, in the remotest parts of the North. I will ascend above the highest clouds; I will make myself like the Most High" (Isaiah 14:13-14).

Lucifer said, "I will ascend ... I will set up my throne ... I will sit ... I will ascend ... I will make." These were decisions that Lucifer made by himself. God did not make the decisions for him, but gave him the freedom to make decisions for himself. In fact, He gives each person and even each angel the freedom to make their own decisions.

God could have created the angels and people like automobiles that are completely controlled by the driver. Then we would go exactly where He wants us to go and do exactly what He wants us to do. We would obey every command that He gives.

But God does not want us to obey because we are forced by Him. He wants us to obey Him because we love Him and choose to obey Him. Therefore He gave us freedom. When you go for prayer or give to the poor, do you do it because someone is forcing you? No, you do it because you love God and believe in Him. These are acts of freedom.

When Lucifer decided to make himself great like God, he sinned against God. So we see that God did not create sin. Lucifer is the creator and father of all sin.

Now heaven is a perfect place, so it is impossible for sin to exist there. If there were one sin in heaven, it would not be perfect anymore and would no longer be heaven. To explain this better, let me give you an example.

Suppose you had a large container of pure, mountain water to offer to guests in your house. The water is clean and pure, just like heaven is clean and pure. But what if I put one small piece of goat droppings in the water and stirred it up. The piece of droppings was very small, but is the water still pure? Would you give it to your guests? Of course not! Even one tiny piece of filth has contaminated the entire container of pure water, just as one sin would contaminate the purity of heaven.

Also understand that God is holy and is a righteous judge. And because He is a good Judge, He must punish sin. Therefore, God sent Lucifer out of heaven. When Lucifer went out, many other angels went with him. At that time, God told them that in the future they would all be punished because of their sin.

Lucifer and the bad angels became God's enemies, and Lucifer's name was changed to Satan, which means "adversary." The bad angels are now called demons. These evil spirits are active all over the earth. They are always trying to oppose God's plans and take glory away from God for themselves.

Part 2: How we became the children of Satan

It is true that Satan is God's enemy, but is God all-powerful? How could Satan ever hurt God? The answer to this comes from the story of Adam and Eve, found in both the Quran and the Bible.

After creating the angels, God created the heavens, the earth, the oceans, the land, and all of the animals. Then God created the first man and woman, Adam and Eve, and placed them in a beautiful garden. In the center of the garden, God placed two special trees: "the tree of life" and "the tree of the knowledge of good and evil." God told Adam and Eve that they could eat the fruit of any tree in the garden, including the tree of life, but they could not eat from the tree of the knowledge of good and evil and if they did eat from it, they would die.

In those days Adam and Eve had a perfect relationship with God. They were able to communicate freely with Him, and there was no disease or death. Also, all of the fruit of the garden grew easily so that there was always enough food to eat.

And this is where Satan hurt God. Since God is all-powerful, Satan could not hurt God directly, so instead, he hurt God by attacking Adam and Eve, whom God loved. It is as if an evil man wanted to hurt you, but he was not strong enough. So he hurt your wife, children, or perhaps your sister instead. Obviously it would cause you great pain to see your loved ones suffer.

This is how it happened. When God sent Satan out of heaven, he went down to the earth in the form of a snake to try to deceive Eve. He said to her, "Did God really say, 'You can't eat from any tree in the garden?'" Of course this was wrong, so Eve explained that they could eat any of the fruit in the garden except the fruit from the tree of the knowledge of good and evil because if they did eat that fruit, they would die.

But Satan lied to Eve and told her that she would not die if she ate the fruit. He said that God did not want her to eat the fruit because it would give her great wisdom, like God himself, and she would know the difference between good and evil.

When Eve heard that the fruit was special and that it would give her great wisdom, she took some of the fruit and ate it. Then she gave the fruit to Adam, and he also ate some.

When Satan wished in his heart to be like God, that was the first sin ever. When Adam and Eve disobeyed God by eating the forbidden fruit, that was the first sin on the earth. Just as God punished Satan for his sin, He also had to punish Adam and Eve.

At this point many people ask, "Since God is merciful, why didn't He just forgive Adam and Eve and not punish them?" Because God is holy and righteous, He must do justice, and this requires punishment for sin. Otherwise, He would not be a good judge.

Imagine that a man killed your brother, and you brought that man before a judge. The murderer confessed his sin, but asked the judge to be merciful. So the judge had mercy upon the man and let him go free. Would this have been right? Would that be a good judge? Of course not. Even though God is merciful, because of His great righteousness, He must punish sin.

So, here is what happened to Adam and Eve. First, God cursed Satan and told him that there would always be trouble between him and people. One day a certain Man would come and completely destroy him. Many prophets wrote about this promised conqueror in the Holy Scriptures, and He is called "The Messiah."

Then God told Adam, "The ground is cursed because of you. You will eat from it by means of painful labor all the days of your life." Just as he threw Satan out of heaven, He also threw Adam and Eve out of the garden and told them that they could never return.

Adam and Eve disobeyed God's command, and their sin has brought the curse upon us all. Now, instead of being born into a perfect world where there is no disease or death and everyone walks closely with God, we are born into a world of war, evil, disease, and death. Because of the sin, we have been separated from God. In fact, we have now become children of Satan rather than of God. People do evil and selfish things, because they listen to Satan and very rarely listen to God.

Before the great sin, there was no death on the earth. Because of the sin, just as God promised to Adam and Eve, every man and woman must die as payment for personal sin. The Bible states this very plainly: "… the wages of sin is death …" (Romans 6:23).

Remember that heaven is perfect, and God cannot allow any sin into heaven. If He did, that sin would destroy the purity of heaven. Since we are all under the curse, we are all sinful in one way or another. This is also stated plainly in the Bible: "… all have sinned and fall short of the glory of God" (Romans 3:23).

When we die, since every human being is a sinner, God cannot allow any of us to come into His perfect heaven. Every human being must join our father, Satan, in hell when we die.

Part 3: How God adopted us into salvation

Just as a person cannot change his parents, we cannot change these facts. The entire world is under a curse, and all people are children of Satan who will join him in hell when they die. Some people know in their hearts that God would be a better father than Satan, and they try to earn their way into God's family by being good. We try to make God happy by praying, fasting, giving money to the poor, or other religious activities. But none of these can take away the curse, change who our father is, or take away our sin. There is nothing that any man can do to earn his or her way into God's family. There is nothing that any man can do to take away a curse placed by God. But God loves each one of us very much. Since God is much stronger than Satan, He has fixed the problem for us.

Since every person with the human spirit is under the curse, God Himself came to earth in the form of a man. Here is how it happened. Thousands of years after the curse began, there was a girl named Mary who had never been with a man. Mary, like every person, was under the curse and lived a very difficult life. But one day, an angel named Gabriel came to her and told her that she would have a child who would be the promised Messiah. The angel said, "He will be great and will be called the Son of the Most High … and His kingdom will have no end."

Mary wanted to know how this could be since she had never been with a man. The angel explained to her that the Holy Spirit would come upon her and, for that reason, the holy child would be called "the Son of God." "For nothing will be impossible for God," Gabriel said. So Mary said that she was God's slave. "May it be done to me according to your word," she said. And it did happen, just as the angel said.

Now, Mary was engaged to a man named Joseph and when he found out that Mary was pregnant, he wanted to break the engage- ment, thinking that Mary had been with a man. But God told Joseph in a dream, "Joseph, son of David, don't be afraid to take Mary as your wife because what has been conceived in her is by the Holy Spirit. She will give birth to a son, and you are to name Him Jesus, because He will save His people from their sins."

On the night that Jesus was born, there were some shepherds with their flocks. That night an angel from God appeared to them, and they were terrified! "Don't be afraid," said the angel. "For look, I proclaim to you good news of great joy that will be for all the people: today a Savior, who is Messiah the Lord, was born for you in the city of David." And suddenly an army of angels was singing, "Glory to God in the highest, and on earth peace, good will toward men."

Because Jesus had been born by God's Spirit, He was not under the curse, and He never committed one sin. He also showed that He had the Spirit of God by doing many great miracles. He made blind people see and paralyzed people walk, cast demons out of people, and even raised people from the dead. One day He was in a boat with His disciples when a great storm came up. The disciples were frightened, because they thought they might drown, but Jesus said to the skies, "Be quiet!" and the storm immediately stopped. This proved that He was the Spirit of God in a man's body because He could command illnesses, demons, death, and even nature.

The religious leaders hated Jesus because they were very jealous of Him. So they arrested Him and ordered that He be killed on a cross. In those days, two large poles were put together to make a cross, and criminals were nailed to it in front of all of the people and were left there until they died. Even though Jesus had never committed one single sin, He was nailed to a cross like this. But this was all a part of God's plan to stop the curse. Jesus was sacrificed for the sins of the world just like a lamb is sacrificed. That is why He is also called "The Lamb of God." While Jesus was on the cross, the sky became very dark, there was a great earthquake, and then Jesus died.

Before Jesus died, He had told His disciples that He was going to die and that He would come back to life after three days. The story sounded crazy, and the disciples didn't believe Him. But on the third day after His death, some women went to the tomb and found that it was empty. An angel appeared to them and explained that Jesus had come back to life, just as He had promised. Over the next 40 days, Jesus appeared to all of His disciples and over 500 other people.

Jesus had brought other people back to life, but all of those people were normal human beings, and they all died again. But Jesus did not die again. He went with His disciples up to a mountain and told them that He had to return to heaven and would send the Holy Spirit of God to each of them to help guide them. His last words were "All authority has been given to Me in heaven and on earth. Go, therefore, and make disciples of all nations, baptizing them in the name of the Father and of the Son and of the Holy Spirit, teaching them to observe everything I have commanded you. And remember, I am with you always, to the end of the age" (Matthew 28:18b-20).

Then Jesus began to float up into the sky and disappeared into the clouds. Two angels appeared next to the disciples and said, "Why do you stand looking up into heaven? This Jesus, who has been taken from you into heaven, will come in the same way that you have seen Him going into heaven."

Part 4: What will happen when Jesus returns?

About a month after Jesus went up to heaven, all of His disciples were sitting together when a loud sound, like a rushing wind, came into the room. Suddenly, little lights, like tongues of fire, appeared above each disciple's head, and they began speaking in many different languages. It was a religious holiday, and visitors were in the town. When Jesus' disciples went outside, the people heard them talking about God in many different languages. They gathered around wondering about this miracle. They kept asking, "These men are not from all of these different nations. How can they speak all of these different languages?"

Then one of the disciples named Peter began to speak to the entire crowd. He explained that Jesus had come from heaven to earth and proved that He was the Spirit of God by doing many miracles. As a part of God's plan, He was killed by the religious leaders, but He rose up from the dead because death could not hold Him. Now that He had returned to heaven, He had sent his Holy Spirit down to His disciples and that was the reason for the miracle of the many languages. When the people heard this, they suddenly realized that Jesus was the Messiah who had come to take the curse away. They wanted to be freed from the curse themselves, and they asked the disciples, "What should we do?"

So Peter explained to them that to become a disciple of Jesus, they must first repent of their sins and be baptized in the name of Jesus. Then they would also receive the Holy Spirit. Peter said that the promise was for them and their children. Even for those who are far away—for everyone that the Lord is calling. Three thousand people became Jesus' disciples that day, and since then, millions of people have become disciples of Jesus. You cannot be born a disciple of Jesus. Each person must decide for himself if he wants to follow Jesus for the rest of his life.

Later, these disciples of Jesus wrote many short books which have been put together to make the New Testament. The New Testament tells many stories about Jesus and explains how God sent Jesus to save us from the curse by being sacrificed for our sins just like a lamb. It is true that we were born as children of Satan, and we can never change that. While we are alive, we will always have to live in Satan's world. But the Bible explains that if we become disciples of Jesus, we will be adopted into God's family. He will give each of us the gift of the Holy Spirit to guide us. This is the free gift of salvation and is a cause for great rejoicing.

Remember that when we were children of Satan, we were destined to join Satan in hell after our death. However, if we become disciples of Jesus and are adopted into God's family, we will go to be with our new Father, God, after we die.

You may ask, but what about our sins? We are still sinful people, and we cannot take our sins into heaven when we die. This is a good point, but when you become a disciple of Jesus, everything changes. It is like this: When each person dies, he goes before God for judgment. If one single sin is found, that person is found guilty and cannot enter into heaven. Remember the example of the tiny piece of goat droppings in the pure water? How do you think God would feel if you offered Him that water to drink, and you told Him that it was good water? Obviously, God would be terribly insulted. In the same way, even if someone's life were 99 percent pure, when he offered himself to God and said that he had lived a good life, this would be a terrible offense to God. The worst thing that a person could do would be to try to rely upon his own good works to impress God. Believe me, when we meet the holy and pure God face to face, we each will know that we are filthy sinners and will fall on our faces in shame.

It is the same way when a disciple of Jesus comes before God for judgment. He or she is also found guilty because of sin. No one can stand as righteous before God. But the Bible tells us that Jesus is always sitting at the right hand of God. When one of His disciples comes before God for judgment, Jesus speaks for us and tells God that He, Jesus, has already paid the penalty for our sins. The payment for sin is death, and Jesus offers the payment of His death for each of His disciples. Since the sins have been paid for by the blood of Jesus, we are found blameless and are able to come into heaven.

At the end of time, Jesus will come back to the earth and will judge everyone who is still alive and everyone who has died. The Bible tells us that He will separate people like sheep and goats. The group that rejected Him will be sent to hell, and the group that believed in Him and became His disciples will be taken up to heaven. Then Jesus will take Satan and all of the demons and throw them into a lake of burning fire where they can never escape.

At the very end of the Bible, it tells us what heaven will be like. It says, "There will no longer be any curse. The throne of God and of the Lamb will be in the city, and His servants will serve Him. They will see His face, and His name will be on their foreheads. Night will no longer exist, and people will not need lamplight or sunlight, because the Lord God will give them light. And they will reign forever and ever."

Please understand that God sent Jesus down to earth because He loves each one of us very much, and He wants us to be adopted into His family. But He will not force anyone. He gives each of us the freedom to accept Jesus or reject Jesus. Now that you know who Jesus really is, you must decide if you believe in Him and want to become His disciple. If you do decide to give the rest of your life to Him, you will also receive the Holy Spirit, and He will never leave you. However, being a disciple of Jesus is also very dangerous. Jesus said that if they persecuted and killed Him, they would also persecute and kill His disciples.

But being a disciple of Jesus will also give you a wonderful peace in your heart. Jesus also said, "Come to Me, all of you who are weary and burdened, and I will give you rest. All of you, take up My yoke and learn from Me, because I am gentle and humble in heart, and you will find rest for yourselves. For My yoke is easy and My burden is light" (Matthew 11:28-30).

NOTES

1. Robert E. Coleman, *The Master Plan of Evangelism*, 2nd ed. (New York: Revell, 1994), 29.

2. K. P. Yohannan, *Revolution in World Missions* Lake Mary, FL: Charisma House, 1995, 109.
To be fair to Brother K. P., it is important to know that he preceded this discussion with the statement, "I am not saying the rich churches in America should stop spending billions of dollars to meet human needs both here and abroad. Yet we must realize we will not even begin to make a dent in the kingdom of darkness until we lift up Christ with all the authority, power, and revelation that is given to us in the Bible."

3. Fundamentalist Baptist Institute, "The Strategy of Preaching," http://www.fbinstitute.com/max/part1.html.

4. C. Daniel Batson and John M. Darley, "'From Jerusalem to Jericho': A Study of Situational and Dispositional Variables in Helping Behavior," *Journal of Personality and Social Psychology* 27 (1973): 100-108.

5. William S. McBirnie, *The Search for the Twelve Apostles* (Carol Stream, IL: Tyndale House, 1979) 294-299.

6. Donald MacGavran, *The Bridges of God* (New York: Friendship Press, 1955), 335-336.

7. Ibid.

8. Global Consultation on World Evangelization, "Great Commission Manifesto," http://www.missionfrontiers.org/1989/0102/jf899.htm.

9. David Garrison, *Church Planting Movements* (Midlothian, VA: Wigtake Resources, 2004), 171-172.

10. The World Revolution, "The State of the World," http://www.worldrevolution.org/projects/globalissuesoverview/overview2/BriefOverview.htm.

11. Ibid.

12. Community Water and Sanitation Facility Cities Alliance, "Partnerships to Deliver Water and Sanitation to the Urban Poor in Slums," http://www.makingcitieswork.org/files/docs/citiesAlliance/ProgramDescription.9.18.pdf.

13. United Nations High Commission on Refugees, (http://www.unhcr.org.)

14. Governance and Social Development Resource Centre, "Penal Reform," http://www.gsdrc.org.

15. USAID, "World TB Day," http://www.usaid.gov/our_work/global_health/id/tuberculosis/news/tbday_2006.html.

16. Burden of Disease Unit, "Risk Factors for Death and Disability," *The Global Burden of Disease and Injury Series*, http://www.hsph.harvard.edu/organizations/bdu/gbdseries_files/gbdsum5.pdf.

17. Urban Jonsson, "Millions Lost to Wrong Strategies," *The Progress of Nations* 1994 (New York: UNICEF, 1994).

18. AVERT.org, "Worldwide HIV and AIDS Statistics," http://www.avert.org/worldstats.html.

19. True Love Waits, http://www.lifeway.com/tlw.

20. T. Yamamori, ed., "Love, Medicine and Prayer in Northwest India," *Serving With the Poor in Asia: Cases in Holistic Ministry* (Monrovia, CA: MARC, 1996), 117-130.

21. World Health Organization. "Maternal mortality in 2005," http://www.who.int/whr/2005/en/.

22. Binava Kumar Bastia and Nilamadhab Kar, "Post-traumatic stress disorder, depression and generalized anxiety in adolescents after natural disaster: a study of comorbidity," *Clinical Practice and Epidemiology in Mental Health*, http://www.pubmedcentral.nih.gov/articlerender.fcgi?artid=1563462.

23. Ravi Jayakaran, "Ten Seed Technique," World Vision China, www.fao.org/participation/Ten-Seed%20Technique-Revised.pdf.

GLOSSARY

AIDS—The disease caused by Human Immunodeficiency Virus (HIV). It is the common abbreviation for Acquired Immunodeficiency Syndrome.

Apostolic—Coming from the Greek word apostolos, it literally means "one who is sent out."

Apostolic worker or minister—A disciple, sent by the church, to make disciples in an area as yet unreached by the Gospel. The word "missionary" is the Latinized form of the word "apostle."

Ascaris lumbricoldes—An intestinal parasite, almost as long as a pencil, that is sometimes passed at defecation.

Christward movement—See disciple movement.

Church—An autonomous group of baptized disciples, associated by covenant in the faith and fellowship of the Gospel, who observe the two ordinances of Christ (baptism and communion); follow His laws; exercise the gifts, rights, and privileges invested in them by His Word; and seek to extend the Gospel to the ends of the earth.

Community—A group of people, not a place, considered as being one.

Community development—The discipline of improving the situation of needy communities through mentoring and teaching.

Contractures—Limited range of motion, often severe, from greatly tightened muscles and tendons.

Cul-de-sac strategy—A disciple-making strategy that plans for less than all three of the components of entering the community, making disciples, and empowering the church.

Disciple—A sworn agent for Christ; the foundation for a healthy church and for disciple movements. Evangelism, disciple making, church formation, and apostolic vision all are inherent in this word.

Disciple making—The active process of producing healthy and replicating agents for Jesus. Every authentic disciple is a disciple maker.

Disciple movement—A sustained multiplicative increase of disciples and churches.

District health officer—In many countries, this is the title for the medical authority of a defined geographic area. This term may vary from country to country.

DOTS—An abbreviation for "Direct Observation Therapy Short-course." This is the currently approved strategy to treat tuberculosis (TB). In this book, the concept of "direct observation therapy" could apply to other diseases that could benefit from frequent monitoring and could use the abbreviation of DOTS for things other than just TB.

Endogenous—Used to describe something generated from within an individual or system.

Exogenous—Used to describe something generated from outside of an individual or system.

Food insecurity—Lack of consistent access to adequate nutrition.

Health strategy—Any disciple-making strategy that involves issues related to water, food, shelter, sanitation, or psychological or physical disease.

HIV—The virus that causes Acquired Immunodeficiency Syndrome (AIDS). It is the common abbreviation for Human Immunodeficiency Virus.

Holistic ministry—Concurrently caring for an individual's and/or community's physical, emotional, social, and spiritual needs.

Home healthcare—Medical or healthcare that is delivered in a patient's home.

Hospice— A program of medical and emotional care for the seriously ill.

Identity compartmentalization—That natural impulse to see and mentally label ourselves according to our education or our job rather than as free agents for Jesus temporarily assigned to live on earth.

Indigenous—Used to describe a native person, persons, or entity.

JESUSfilm—A two-hour docudrama about the life of Christ based on the Gospel of Luke. The film, distributed by Campus Crusade for Christ, has been seen in every country of the world and translated into hundreds of languages since its initial release in 1979.

Language group—A group of people who share the same language.

Lay leadership—Leadership coming from disciples who are not necessarily trained or paid for service. These people have non-church-related jobs and lead because of their love for Jesus.

Long-term personnel—Apostolic workers, sent by the church, with a long-term commitment to start churches of disciples.

Malnutrition—Improper nutrition due to a lack of enough food or a lack of the right kinds of food. Technically, eating too much food is also "malnutrition."

Man of peace—Based upon Luke 10:6, this individual is prepared by God to receive apostolic workers. He or she often has influence in the community and will readily pave the way for the team's ministry. Because this individual can be either gender, the term "person of peace" is sometimes used.

Medical strategy—A health strategy that requires at least one medically trained team member. In some strategies, this person can be hired from the local or nearby community.

Midwifery—Assisting a woman through childbirth. A "midwife" is a highly trained medical practitioner in the discipline of midwifery.

Ministry of Health—The authority, related to health issues, over entire regions. Many district health officers may report to one minister of health.

Missionary—See apostolic worker.

Nation—Biblically this word comes from the Greek word "ethnos" and is also translated as "Gentiles," depending upon the context. The term does not refer to modern nations as defined by current borders, but by ethnic groups. The Kurds, Arabs, or Pueblo Indians are all examples of "nations."

National—A native of the local area. An American is a national of the United States but is an "expatriate" when living in another country.

Non-doctor—Any person who has avoided the acquisition of a medical degree.

Occupational therapy—A form of rehabilitation focusing on improving activities of daily living.

Palliative care—Easing the severity of pain of a disease without removing the cause.

People movement—See disciple movement.

Physical therapy—Treatment of musculo-skeletal maladies, whether congenital or acquired, without the use of surgery or medicine.

Platform—One's identity as perceived by the community and the foundation upon which one makes disciples.

Prayerwalking—The simple act of walking through a community and praying for whatever comes to mind as one sees people, homes, and offices.

Preaching—Verbal transfer of the Gospel to an audience of any size.

Rehabilitation—Restoration to useful life through education and therapy.

Scabies—An itching rash caused by a tiny parasite that burrows under one's skin.

Social services—Ministry to physical, emotional, moral, community, educational, or financial needs.

Speech therapy—The treatment of maladies related to speech or swallowing.

Strategy—A thought-out plan to enter a community, make disciples, and empower the church. A good strategy can and should include the component of divine assistance.

Synergy—The collaboration of two or more disciples to produce a kingdom effect greater than could be achieved by a disciple acting alone.

Tactics—Methods or projects that make up one's strategy.

Traditional birthing attendant (TBA)—Not a midwife but an attendant at a birth. TBAs can receive a wide range of training, but they are not considered skilled birthing practitioners.

True Love Waits—A teaching program, aimed at young people, that advocates and encourages a signed commitment to abstain from sex until marriage.

Tuberculosis (TB)—A deadly and contagious disease caused by a germ. It most often affects the lungs but can affect any body system.

Two white guys (TWGs)—An apostolic team made up of two Western (and in this case, white) expatriates. Although this team may be very effective, it is generally best for teams to be made first of nationals, then of nationals plus expatriates, and lastly, of two expatriates or TWGs.

Underdeveloped or undeveloped world—Those places where people live in relative poverty, generally without an opportunity to improve their socioeconomic standing, regardless of ability or hard work.

Unengaged people group—Any people group without an evangelical church-planting methodology being implemented.

Volunteer—Partners in apostolic work serving for weeks or months at personal cost.

Wellness—State of being well.

World Food Program—Branch of the United Nations responsible for providing food aid to those in need. It is the largest humanitarian agency.

World Health Organization (WHO)—Branch of the United Nations responsible for improving health around the world.

ADDITIONAL RESOURCES

Related to being a disciple:

Chambers, Oswald. *My Utmost for His Highest*. Toronto: The Canadian
   Publishers, 1935.
This is a book of daily devotions that will resonate with the Holy
Spirit within a disciple.

Coleman, Robert E. *The Master Plan of Evangelism.* 2nd ed. Grand
   Rapids, MI: Revell, 1995.
Although this is written purely for preachers, it is guaranteed to
motivate any disciple to become a disciple maker.

MacArthur, John. *The Gospel According to Jesus*. Grand Rapids, MI:
   Zondervan, 1994.
This is an excellent treatise on a disciple's complete abandonment
to the agenda of Jesus.

Piper, John. *Let the Nations Be Glad! The Supremacy of God in Missions*.
   Grand Rapids, MI: Baker Books, 1993.
I know of no other book that better explains the inherent apostolic
nature of authentic disciples. It also dips into apostolic strategy by
giving the biblical basis for the "A" of the ABCs strategy.

Rankin, Jerry and Phyllis Tadlock. *Impact Your World: Basic Training
   for Mission Teams*. Nashville: LifeWay Press, 2006.
I recommend using this book and DVD as a part of a rigorous orien-
tation process before short-term volunteers leave home.

Related to church planting:

Neighbor, Ralph W. Jr. *Where Do We Go From Here?: A Guidebook for the Cell Group Church*. Houston: Touch Publication, 2000.
This is still my favorite book on a more replicable church.

Simson, Wolfgang. *Houses that Change the World*. Carlisle, UK: Paternoster Publishing, 2001.
This should be at least one of the books you read concerning the form of church that is more conducive to replication.

Related to overall missions strategy:

Allen, Roland. *Missionary Methods: St. Paul's or Ours?* Grand Rapids, MI: Wm. B. Eerdmans Publishing Co., 1962.
This insightful book looks at many different aspects of apostolic strategy.

Winter, Ralph and Steve Hawthorne, eds. *Perspectives on the World Christian Movement*. 3rd ed. Pasadena, CA: William Carey Library, 1999.
This book is a compilation of over 100 articles designed to teach the reader why and how we do effective missions.

Help for specific health-strategy development:

HIV/AIDS strategy
True Love Waits, http://www.lifeway.com/tlw/.
This is the American website for "True Love Waits," the program that educates youth to abstain from sex until marriage. Its usage in HIV endemic areas has been identified as an important component in national anti-HIV strategies.

The rehabilitation strategy

March of Dimes. "The March of Dimes Global Report on Birth Defects." 2008. http://www.marchofdimes.com/professionals/871_18587. asp.

This is their official report on birth defects internationally.

Werner, David. *Disabled Village Children*. (Berkeley, CA,: The Hesperian Foundation, 1999). http://www.dinf.ne.jp/doc/english/global/ david/dwe002/dwe00201.htm.

This is a wonderful online book that can teach a team all about rehabilitation at the grassroots level.

Hospice strategy

Wright, Michael, Justin Wood, Tom Lynch, David Clark. "Mapping levels of palliative care development: a global view." *International Observatory on End of Life Care* (Lancaster, NY: National Hospice and Palliative Care Organization, 2006). www.nhpco.org/files/public/palliativecare/world_map_report_final-0107.pdf.

This is a PDF document that reports the prevalence of hospice and palliative care around the world.

Help for community development:

Jayakaran, Ravi. "Ten Seed Technique." 2002. www.fao.org/participation/Ten-Seed%20Technique-Revised.pdf.

This is a large, color PDF document that will teach you all about the "Ten Seed Technique," a very useful Participative Learning and Action (PLA) skill discussed in Appendix C.

LifeWind International, http://www.lifewind.org.

This organization provides excellent community development training called "Community Health Education."

Medical Missions Response. www.mmronline.org.
This is an organization, which I co-founded, that sends skilled medical volunteers to work directly in health/church-planting strategies among the most overlooked people groups.

Rowland, Stan. *Multiplying Light and Truth through Community Health Evangelism.* **Pant Nagar, Mumbai: GLS Publishing, 2001.**
Community Health Evangelism (CHE) is a holistic community development strategy that has been used effectively around the world.

Werner, David. *Where There is No Doctor.* **Palo Alto, CA: The Hesperian Foundation, 1992.**
This is the book we use to prepare a health lesson for community health workers.